Colloquial
French

THE COLLOQUIAL SERIES
Series Adviser: Gary King

The following languages are available in the Colloquial series:

Afrikaans	German	Romanian
Albanian	Greek	Russian
Amharic	Gujarati	Scottish Gaelic
Arabic (Levantine)	Hebrew	Serbian
Arabic of Egypt	Hindi	Slovak
Arabic of the Gulf	Hungarian	Slovene
Basque	Icelandic	Somali
Bengali	Indonesian	Spanish
Breton	Irish	Spanish of Latin
Bulgarian	Italian	America
Burmese	Japanese	Swahili
Cambodian	Kazakh	Swedish
Cantonese	Korean	Tamil
Catalan	Latvian	Thai
Chinese (Mandarin)	Lithuanian	Tibetan
Croatian	Malay	Turkish
Czech	Mongolian	Ukrainian
Danish	Norwegian	Urdu
Dutch	Panjabi	Vietnamese
English	Persian	Welsh
Estonian	Polish	Yiddish
Finnish	Portuguese	Yoruba
French	Portuguese of Brazil	Zulu (forthcoming)

COLLOQUIAL 2s series: *The Next Step in Language Learning*

Chinese	German	Russian
Dutch	Italian	Spanish
French	Portuguese of Brazil	Spanish of Latin America

Colloquials are now supported by FREE AUDIO available online. All audio tracks referenced within the text are free to stream or download from www.routledge.com/cw/colloquials. If you experience any difficulties accessing the audio on the companion website, or still wish to purchase a CD, please contact our customer services team through www.routledge.com/info/contact.

Colloquial
French

The Complete Course for Beginners

Valérie Demouy and
Alan Moys

Routledge
Taylor & Francis Group

LONDON AND NEW YORK

First published 2006
by Routledge
2 Park Square, Milton Park, Abingdon, Oxon, OX14 4RN

Simultaneously published in the USA and Canada
by Routledge
711 Third Avenue, New York, NY 10017

Routledge is an imprint of the Taylor & Francis Group, an informa business

© 2006 New material Valérie Demouy, material from
previous edition Alan Moys

First edition published 1996 by Routledge

Reprinted 1997, 1998, 1999, 2001, 2003

© 1996 Alan Moys

British Library Cataloguing in Publication Data
A catalogue record for this book is available from the British Library

Library of Congress Cataloging in Publication Data
Demouy, Valérie, 1964–
   Colloquial French: the complete course for beginners/
Valérie Demouy and Alan Moys. – 3rd ed.
      p. cm – (The colloquial series)
   Moys appears as sole author of first ed.
   Includes indexes.
   1. French language – Conversation and phrase books –
English.   2. French language – Spoken French.
   I. Moys, Alan.   II. Title.   III. Series.
   PC2121.M85 2005
   448.3′421 – dc22   2005008589

ISBN: 978-1-138-94968-3 (pbk)

Typeset in Times by
Florence Production Ltd, Stoodleigh, Devon

Contents

Acknowledgements

The author would like to thank Professor Jim Coleman, Marie-Noëlle Lamy and Annie Eardley (The Open University) for their support during the production of this book and Nadine Gilbert, Josette Demouy, Annie Eardley and Morgan Jones for providing some of the photographs. Special thanks to Steve Pidcock (University of Warwick) for his unfailing confidence, support and invaluable critical reading. This book is dedicated to my parents and Steve Pidcock.

Valérie Demouy

Introduction

Colloquial French is intended for adult beginners who have little or no prior knowledge of French. It has been designed in such a way that it can be used in adult education classes or by learners who wish to study at home at their own pace and in their own time.

Colloquial French covers the basic structures and the vocabulary of everyday situations which you are likely to encounter, whether on holiday or on business in France and in other French-speaking countries. Its emphasis is on spoken French and its primary aim is to develop your communication skills.

The language is approached in a functional and communicative way so that you can easily use what you have learned to communicate in French effectively. We have kept the grammatical explanations as simple and user-friendly as possible to allow you to progress at a steady pace but at the same time build up a sound understanding of how the language works and so build up your confidence.

Colloquial French comprises a book and accompanying audio material which can be freely downloaded from www.routledge.com/cw/colloquials. This audio contains recordings of the dialogues with oral activities.

How is the course organised?

There are eighteen units, normally laid out in the same way. At the beginning of the book, you will find a pronunciation guide and at the end, the key to the exercises, a reference grammar, a French–English glossary and two indexes.

What is in a unit?

Dialogues

There are normally two per unit. Their main function is to introduce the key points of the unit, in context, and in a way that the
French would use them. They are also essential for developing your
listening and speaking skills.

In Units 1–8, the French dialogues are immediately followed by
their translation into English. From Unit 9 onwards, a glossary of
new vocabulary is provided instead.

Language points

Under functional (e.g.: *expressing preferences*) or grammatical
headings (e.g.: *using y*) are given clear and concise explanations of
new structures, together with examples. Grammatical terms and
explanations have been simplified and kept to a minimum so that
you can understand the mechanisms underpinning structures and
use them successfully and confidently.

Exercises

These follow the language points and provide you with lots of
practice in the new structures you are learning. Some of the exercises are also recorded on the CD/cassettes. There is a key to the
exercises at the end of the book.

Other features

In some units, and when useful, we have included some *cultural
points* about France. We have also included some short texts
covering topics in some units. These texts contain some of the
language learned and are there to provide you with further examples of the language, as well as to start developing your reading
skills.

The recordings and how to work with them

The recordings contain the dialogues and a variety of exercises designed to improve your pronunciation, intonation and communication skills.

When you first listen to a dialogue, try not to look at the transcription of the dialogue or the translation. Focus your listening on the following questions. Who is talking? Where is the dialogue taking place? What is the purpose of the conversation? If you need to, listen to the recording again, until you can answer those three questions. Then listen again and focus on words you can recognise or understand. Write them down and try to make sensible guesses about what you don't understand yet. Then check your guesses by listening and reading at the same time. Avoid looking at the translation until you are happy you've tested yourself as much as you can. Approaching listening activities, and particularly the dialogues in this way, will initially take time. But as you progress through the course, it will become second nature and will take far less time. You will then acquire a growing confidence in your ability to understand native French speakers and will be more successful in communicating with them.

You can further improve your listening and oral skills by listening repeatedly to the recordings, even and especially if they are related to units you have already studied. You can do this in your car or while you are doing something else. The more you listen to the language, the easier it will become to understand what is being said. Because your ear will become more and more accustomed to hearing French, you will not only memorise the structures and vocabulary more effectively, but you will also improve your pronunciation and intonation. You should also use the recordings to practise your pronunciation and intonation by repeating what you hear.

General learning tips

Learning a language is not difficult but requires time, patience and dedication. It's usually better for learners to work often (say three to four times a week) and for short periods of time (30–40 minutes) rather than plan to do two hours every weekend. So, don't be too ambitious with the goals you set for yourself. A realistic timetable of when you can work on your language will avoid frustrations and disappointments.

It's often difficult to keep motivation going if you learn on your own. Try to find someone to work with. It's generally more motivating to learn a language together with someone else. Remember that there are lots of activities in the course that easily lend themselves to role-playing. Make the most of them if you are learning with someone else and above all enjoy yourself.

Bon courage!

Pronunciation guide

The sounds

These are often not too difficult to master, with a little practice. It might be useful to learn the phonetic transcription of the sounds of French, especially if you intend to go beyond this book. You can then find out how a word is pronounced by looking it up in a good bilingual or monolingual French dictionary. Each entry will have its phonetic transcription. Here, we have given both the phonetic transcription of most French sounds and, whenever there is one, a nearest English equivalent.

In the following section square brackets denote a symbol from the International Phonetic Alphabet (IPA).

Vowels

IPA	French examples	Nearest English equivalents
[a]	taxi, ami, chat	cat, tap
[i]	vie, dit, lycée	sleep, tea (but shorter)
[u]	vous, pour, nous	you, fool (but shorter)
[y]	tu, rue, plus	*no equivalent*
[e]	thé, aller, chez	a cross between fit, pin and jelly, tepid
[ɛ]	faire, mère, belle	fair, mare
[o]	mot, beau, moto	raw (but shorter)
[ɔ]	port, homme, donne	porridge, olive
[œ]	peur, leur, meuble	fur, purr
[ø]	peu, veux, deux	*no equivalent*
[ə] or [(ə)]	premier, ce, le	perform, preparation

Tips for pronouncing [y], [ø] and [o]

- for [y] and [ø], your lips should be forward, making an O shape (rather like for a kiss!)
- for [y], start with the sound [i]
- for [ø], start with the sound [ə]
- for [o], your tongue should be more forward in your mouth than for [ɔ], your lips more forward and your mouth less open.

The four nasalised vowels

There are no English equivalents for these. They originate from the basic vowels [a], [ɔ], [ε] and [œ], which means that, in effect, the position of the tongue and the lips and the opening of the mouth are the same as for the basic vowels. They are called nasalised because the air used to pronounce them partly travels through the nasal cavities. Check whether you are saying them correctly, by feeling to see if there is a little vibration when you pinch lightly just below the bridge of your nose.

[ã]   ba**n**c, ve**n**t, te**m**ps, **am**phithéâtre
[ɔ̃]   lo**ng**, so**m**bre
[ε̃]   vi**n**, améric**ain**, pl**ein**, f**aim**
[œ̃]   lu**n**di, parf**um**

[œ̃] is only pronounced in the south of France. It becomes [ε̃] as soon as you move northwards, above the Massif Central.

When **an**, **en**, **em**, **on**, **om**, **in**, **ain**, **ein**, **aim**, **un**, **um** are followed by a vowel or another **n** or **m**, they are not pronounced as nasals:

J'**aime** le chocolat
Monaco
Une Itali**enne**
Une ann**ée**

Consonants

IPA	French examples	Nearest English equivalents
[p]	**p**apa, **p**artir, a**pp**artement	**P**eter, **p**ort
[t]	**t**hé, **t**arte, vi**t**e	**t**ea, **t**enor

[k]	copie, **qu**i, **k**ayak	**k**eep, **c**olour
[b]	**b**on, **b**éret, a**bb**aye	**b**eep, **b**oat
[d]	**d**épart, ai**d**e, a**d**orer	**d**eep, a**d**apt
[g]	**g**are, al**gu**e, **g**ondole	**g**orilla, **g**arbage
[f]	télé**ph**oner, **f**ils, **f**amille	**f**ire, **ph**one
[s]	i**c**i, **ç**a, de**ss**ert, **s**el, na**t**ion	**s**alt, **s**ell
[ʃ]	**ch**er, va**ch**e, a**ch**eter	**fi**sh, me**sh**
[v]	**v**ous, a**v**ec, **v**erre	**v**ery, **v**intage
[z]	**z**éro, fai**s**ons, dé**s**ert	de**s**ert, Pi**s**a
[ʒ]	**j**e, **g**îte, **G**eorges	plea**s**ure, lei**s**ure
[l]	se**l**, **l**entement, **l**it	**l**ife, **l**et
[r]	**r**ue, p**r**og**r**amme, Pa**r**is	*no equivalent*
[m]	**m**on, **m**ère, **m**ontagne	**m**other, **m**erry
[n]	**n**on, an**n**ée, **N**îmes	**n**o, **n**ever
[ɲ]	vi**gn**e, A**gn**ès, a**gn**eau	an**n**ual

Tips on pronouncing the sound [r]

It is pronounced at the back of the mouth, rather like when you are trying to clear your throat! Try it on its own first and then with a vowel sound before it:

tard
tort
terre
fort

Once you think you are near enough, try to do it with a vowel after it:

rue
retard
rôti
rapide

Spelling and sounds

In French, the way a word is spelled is often enough to know how it is pronounced. Here are the most basic rules that are useful to memorise.

The letter 'c'

– is pronounced [k] in front of the letters **a**, **o** and **u**:

   cadeau, **c**ou, **c**ure

– is pronounced [s] in front of the letters **e**, **i** and **y**:

   cela, **c**ite, **c**ygne

– **c** + **h** are normally pronounced [ʃ]:

   chat, **ch**er, **ch**ute

– **c** + **h** are sometimes pronounced [k]:

   psy**ch**ose, **ch**arisme

Note that **ç** is always pronounced [s] and used in front of the letters **a**, **o** and **u**:

   ça, les A**ç**ores

The letter 'g'

– is pronounced [g] in front of the letters **a**, **o** and **u**:

   gare, **g**orille, **g**uerre

– is pronounced [ʒ] in front of the letters **e** and **i**:

   gérer, **g**îte

The letter 's'

– is normally pronounced [z] when it is placed in between two vowels:

   dé**s**ert, i**s**otherme, pha**s**e

– is normally pronounced [s] in all other cases:

   statistique, **s**ocial

Note that the letters 'ss' are used in between two vowels to produce the sound [s]:

   de**ss**ert, a**ss**ocier

The letter 'e'

Is normally pronounced [ε] in front of a double consonant:

belle, terre, prennent

Accents and sounds

Accents in French can be disconcerting for a learner, but they are important, because, in a lot of cases, they will give you the key to how a word is pronounced and will also help to differentiate between words which are nearly identical but have different meanings.

Compare:

marche	walking, working
marché	market, walked

The following accents can be found on the letters **a**, **e**, **i**, **o** and **u**:

accent aigu	acute accent
` **accent grave**	grave accent
^ **accent circonflexe**	circumflex accent

- With the letters **a**, **i**, **o** and **u**, you can find the **accent grave** and **circonflexe**, which generally do not alter the sound of the vowel.
- With the letter **e**, you can find all three accents; **-é** is always pronounced [e]; **-è** is always pronounced [ε]; **-ê** can be pronounced [e] or [ε].

1 Premiers contacts

First contacts

In this unit you will learn about:

- greetings
- the verb **être**
- some regular **-er** verbs to talk about yourself
- **ne . . . pas**
- **quel/quelle** to ask questions
- numbers 1–60
- adjectives of nationality

Dialogue 1 🎧 (Audio 1; 1)

Dans le taxi

In the taxi

Anne Murdoch arrives in Belzain, a French town, and takes a taxi to her hotel. Try to understand what we learn about her.

ANNE:	Bonjour, monsieur. Hôtel Les Lilas, s'il vous plaît.
CHAUFFEUR:	Hôtel Les Lilas? On y va, madame. Vous êtes anglaise?
ANNE:	Non, je suis écossaise, mais j'habite en Angleterre.
CHAUFFEUR:	A Londres?
ANNE:	Non, je travaille à Londres, mais j'habite à Coventry.
CHAUFFEUR:	Vous parlez bien français!
ANNE:	Merci. C'est gentil!

CHAUFFEUR:	Voilà, on est arrivé. Ça fait 8 euros, madame.
ANNE:	Voilà. Merci beaucoup, monsieur. Au revoir.
CHAUFFEUR:	Au revoir et bon séjour!

ANNE:	*Hello. Hotel Les Lilas, please.*
TAXI-DRIVER:	*Hotel Les Lilas? OK. Are you English?*
ANNE:	*No, I'm Scottish but I live in England.*
TAXI-DRIVER:	*In London?*
ANNE:	*No, I work in London but I live in Coventry.*
TAXI-DRIVER:	*You speak good French!*
ANNE:	*Thank you. That's very kind!*
TAXI-DRIVER:	*Here we are. That's 8 euros.*
ANNE:	*Here you are. Thank you very much. Goodbye.*
TAXI-DRIVER:	*Goodbye and enjoy your stay!*

Language points

Greetings and opening moves 🎧 (Audio 1; 2)

The French use **monsieur** and **madame** much more frequently than speakers of English use *sir* and *madam*. Note how Anne greets the taxi-driver and how he says goodbye to her.

Bonjour, monsieur.   **Au revoir, madame.**

Bonsoir is used in the evening, both when you greet people and when you leave.

Bonsoir, monsieur.   **Bonsoir, madame.**

Salut is more informal and is used between people who generally know each other well. It is also used both to greet people and when you leave.

Salut Pierre!   **Salut Martine!**

Politeness is also greatly appreciated in France. The French will normally say **bonjour**, **au revoir** and **merci** when entering and leaving a shop, even if they just go in to have a look. Do not forget to say **s'il vous plaît** when asking for something.

Un café, s'il vous plaît.
Merci.

Talking about nationalities 🎧 (Audio 1; 3)

To ask about Anne's nationality, the taxi-driver said:

Vous êtes anglaise?

She answered:

Non, je suis écossaise.

To give your nationality in French, you say if you are a man:	*To give your nationality in French, you say if you are a woman:*	
Je suis anglais.	**Je suis anglaise.**	(I am English)
Je suis français.	**Je suis française.**	(I am French)
Je suis écossais.	**Je suis écossaise.**	(I am Scottish)
Je suis hollandais.	**Je suis hollandaise.**	(I am Dutch)

Note that the pronunciation changes as well as the spelling. Here are some more examples:

Je suis américain.	**Je suis américaine.**	(American)
Je suis italien.	**Je suis italienne.**	(Italian)
Je suis allemand.	**Je suis allemande.**	(German)

Sometimes, the spelling might change but the pronunciation will stay the same:

Je suis espagnol.	**Je suis espagnole.**	(Spanish)

Note that, generally, the mark of the feminine is an **-e**.

But when the adjective of nationality already ends in **-e** in its masculine form, it remains unchanged in its feminine form:

Je suis belge.	**Je suis belge.**	(Belgian)
Je suis russe.	**Je suis russe.**	(Russian)

Did you notice?

Adjectives of nationality in French do not have a capital letter. Capital letters are used only:

- for the names of countries, e.g. **la France**, **l'Angleterre**;
- for the noun when it refers to the people of a country, e.g. **un Italien** (an Italian), **une Anglaise** (an Englishwoman). When it

refers to a language, there is no capital letter, e.g. **l'espagnol** (Spanish), **le russe** (Russian).

The verb être (to be)

Je **suis** italien/italienne.	I am Italian
Tu **es** espagnol/espagnole.	You (informal) are Spanish.
Il **est** français.	He is French.
Elle **est** française.	She is French.
Nous **sommes** en vacances.	We are on holiday.
Vous **êtes** en vacances?	Are you on holiday?
Ils **sont** à Londres.	They are in London.
Elles **sont** à Paris.	They are in Paris.

Note that **elles** represents a group of women only whereas **ils** will include at least one man.

Exercice 1

Fill in the gaps with the correct form of **être**.

1 Vous _____ français? Non, je _____ suisse.
2 Ils _____ anglais.
3 *Le Monde* _____ un journal français.
4 Nous _____ belges mais nous habitons à Paris.
5 Tu _____ espagnole?
6 Elle _____ italienne.

Exercice 2

Answer the following questions about the nationality of the following people.

> *Example*: **Winston Churchill est américain?**
> **Non, il est anglais.**

1 Madonna est anglaise?
2 Tchaïkovsky est belge?
3 Juliette Binoche est italienne?
4 Pedro Almodóvar est russe?
5 Et vous? Vous êtes français(e)?

Language points

Asking questions

The simplest way to ask a question in French is to use intonation. When asking a question, your voice must have a rising intonation at the end of the sentence to distinguish it from a statement.

Vous êtes français.   (statement)

Vous êtes français?   (question)

Did you notice?

When the taxi-driver asked Anne if she was English, he said:

Vous êtes anglaise?
‿
z

This is called a liaison. Liaisons are a feature of French pronunciation. There are some rules, but the easiest way is to try to imitate what you hear as much as you can.

Giving more information about yourself

Anne is Scottish, but what else do we know about her?

Elle *habite* en Angleterre, à Coventry.
She lives in England, in Coventry.

Elle *travaille* à Londres.
She works in London.

Elle *parle* bien français.
She speaks good French.

Verbs in French change their form according to the person (**je**, **tu**, **il**, **elle**, etc.) they are used with. This is called conjugation. We have provided you with more information on how verbs are conjugated in the reference grammar.

Habiter, **travailler** and **parler** are **-er** verbs, so-called because their infinitive (the form under which you will find them in any dictionary) ends in **-er**. Most **-er** verbs are regular in the way that they change their form according to the person (**je, tu, il, elle,** etc.) they are used with. Since most French verbs are **-er** verbs, it is useful to try to memorise the model below. For regular **-er** verbs such as **travailler**, you simply need to take off the **-er** and add the endings as shown.

The verb travailler (to work)

Je travaill	**e**		Nous travaill	**ons**
Tu travaill	**es**		Vous travaill	**ez**
Il travaill	**e**		Ils travaill	**ent**
Elle travaill	**e**		Elles travaill	**ent**

Note that **je** will drop its **e** in front of a vowel or an **h** e.g. **j'habite**. The forms **travaille, travailles** and **travaillent** are pronounced in the same way.

Here are a few other verbs which work in exactly the same way:

téléphoner	to phone	**écouter**	to listen
regarder	to look	**arriver**	to arrive
aimer	to like/love		

You should practise conjugating them.

Exercise 3 🎧 (Audio 1; 5)

Answer the following questions about Anne Murdoch, making full sentences.

1 Elle est anglaise?
2 Elle habite à Londres?
3 Elle travaille à Coventry?
4 Elle parle français?

Now answer these questions:

5 Vous êtes écossais(e)?
6 Vous habitez à Londres?
7 Vous travaillez à Londres?
8 Vous parlez anglais?

Language points

Did you notice?

Anne travaille *en* **Angleterre.**
Elle habite *à* **Coventry.**

The French will usually use **à** in front of the name of a town and **en** in front of the name of a country.

J'habite *en* **France,** *à* **Courchevel, mais je travaille** *en* **Suisse.**
I live in France, in Courchevel, but I work in Switzerland.

However, you will find that **à**, **au**, and **aux** will sometimes be used in front of names of countries. More information will be given in Unit 5.

Dialogue 2 🎧 (Audio 1; 6)

A l'hôtel

At the hotel

Anne Murdoch checks in at the reception desk of her hotel.

ANNE:	Bonsoir monsieur, j'ai une réservation pour quatre nuits.
RECEPTIONNISTE:	Quel est votre nom, s'il vous plaît, madame?
ANNE:	Anne Murdoch.
RECEPTIONNISTE:	Comment ça s'écrit?
ANNE:	M-U-R-D-O-C-H. C'est un nom écossais.
RECEPTIONNISTE:	Ah, vous n'êtes pas anglaise, alors!
ANNE:	Non, je ne suis pas anglaise mais écossaise.
RECEPTIONNISTE:	Un moment, s'il vous plaît . . . je ne trouve pas votre nom. Vous n'êtes pas sur ma liste, on dirait . . . Ah, si! Excusez-moi. Anne Murdoch, voilà. Signez cette fiche s'il vous plaît, madame.
ANNE:	Quelle est la date aujourd'hui?
RECEPTIONNISTE:	Nous sommes le 20, madame.
ANNE:	Voilà, monsieur.
RECEPTIONNISTE:	Merci, madame. Votre chambre est la 12 au premier étage.

ANNE:	*Good evening. I have booked a room for four nights.*
RECEPTIONIST:	*What is your name?*
ANNE:	*Anne Murdoch.*
RECEPTIONIST:	*How do you spell that?*
ANNE:	*M-U-R-D-O-C-H. It's a Scottish name.*
RECEPTIONIST:	*So, you are not English, then.*
ANNE:	*No, I'm not English but Scottish.*
RECEPTIONIST:	*One moment please ... I can't find your name. It seems you are not on my list ... Ah, yes! I'm sorry. Anne Murdoch, here. Please sign this form.*
ANNE:	*What's the date today?*
RECEPTIONIST:	*It's the 20th.*
ANNE:	*Here you are.*
RECEPTIONIST:	*Thank you. Your room is number 12, on the first floor.*

Language points

Spelling things out loud 🎧 (Audio 1; 7)

The French alphabet is the same as the English but is pronounced differently. You may have to spell your name and the following explains how you do this.

The vowels

a	as in **pl*a*t**	**o**	as in **b*eau***
e	as in **f*eu***	**u**	as in **r*ue***
i	as in **v*i*lle**	**y**	is pronounced ***i grec***

The consonants

b	as in **b*é*b*é***	**h**	as in **va*ch*e**
c	as in **c'est**	**j**	as in **g*î*te**
d	as in **d*é*part**	**k**	as in **c*a*deau**
f	as in **gre*ff*e**	**l**	as in **e*ll*e**
g	as in **man*g*é**	**m**	as in **ai*m*e**

n	as in **Hél*è*n*e***	**t**	as in ***thé***
p	**as *p*aix**	**v**	as in ***v*eto**
q	as in ***cu*isine**	**w**	is pronounced ***double v***
r	as in **m*è*re**	**x**	as in **fi*x*e**
s	as in **pr*esse***	**z**	is pronounced ***zède***

A double letter would be said like this:

Harrison: H-A-deux R-I-S-O-N

Did you notice how the receptionist asked Anne to spell her name?

Comment ça s'écrit?
(literally) How is it written?

You can also say:
Vous pouvez épeler, s'il vous plaît?
Can you spell it, please?

Exercise 4 🎧 (Audio 1; 8)

Try spelling out loud the following names.

Murdoch
Beethoven
Leicester
Birmingham

Language points 🎧 (Audio 1; 9)

Start counting

0	**zéro**		
1	**un, une**	11	**onze**
2	**deux**	12	**douze**
3	**trois**	13	**treize**
4	**quatre**	14	**quatorze**
5	**cinq**	15	**quinze**
6	**six**	16	**seize**
7	**sept**	17	**dix-sept**
8	**huit**	18	**dix-huit**
9	**neuf**	19	**dix-neuf**
10	**dix**	20	**vingt**

From 20 to 60, it works like this:

20	**vingt**
21	**vingt et un(e)**
22	**vingt-deux**
23	**vingt-trois**

And so on.

| 30 | **trente** |
| 31 | **trente et un(e)** |

And so on.

40	**quarante**
50	**cinquante**
60	**soixante**

Phone numbers are usually made up of ten digits. They are normally pronounced in five pairs of numbers, like this:

05. 59. 66. 20. 17
zéro cinq; cinquante-neuf; soixante-six; vingt; dix-sept

Exercise 5

What is your room number? Say the numbers out loud.

24   5   19   32   50   49   11   16   6

How much was your taxi fare? Say the fares out loud.

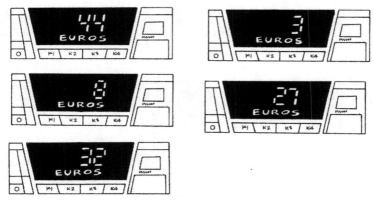

44 euros   8 euros   32 euros   3 euros   27 euros

Language points

Asking for more information

You can use **quel/quelle est** to request more information.

Quel est **votre nom?**	*Quelle est* **votre adresse?**
What's your name?	What's your address?
Quel est **le numéro de votre chambre?**	*Quelle est* **votre profession?**
What's your room number?	What's your profession?

Quel will change to **quelle** when the noun it is associated with is feminine.

Quel est *le problème*?	*Quelle* est *la solution*?
What's the problem?	What's the solution?

Exercise 6

Match each question with its correct answer.

1	Quel est votre nom, s'il vous plaît?	(a)	20 avenue du Loup, Bizanos
2	Comment ça s'écrit?	(b)	Mme Villard
3	Quelle est votre adresse?	(c)	05. 59. 34. 54. 32
4	Quel est votre numéro de téléphone?	(d)	V-I-deux L-A-R-D

Now, imagine you are asking this person for the information given on his card.

Nom: *Pierre Durand*
Nationalité: *Belge*
Adresse: *32 rue de la Libération*
64000 Pau
Tel: *05 59 34 54 32*
Profession: *journaliste*

Language points

Using ne . . . pas

Vous êtes anglaise?   Are you English?
Non, je *ne* suis *pas* anglaise. No, I'm not English.

Je *ne* trouve *pas* votre nom. I can't find your name.
Vous *n'*êtes *pas* sur ma liste. You are not on my list.

Ne ... pas is placed on either side of the verb. **Ne** drops the **e** in front of **a vowel** or an **h**.

Vous *n'*êtes *pas* anglaise?
Anne Murdoch *n'*habite *pas* en Ecosse.

Exercise 7

Here is a profile of you. How accurate is it? Whenever it is not, turn the statement into a negative sentence.

1 Je suis français(e).
2 J'habite à Lille.
3 Je travaille à Londres.
4 Je parle anglais.
5 Je suis journaliste.

2 Dans la ville

In town

In this unit you will learn about:

- how to ask for facilities
- locating places and asking for directions
- a few more **-er** verbs
- **avoir** and **il y a**
- the gender of nouns
- using **un/une** and **le/la**
- numbers 60–1000

Dialogue 1 (Audio 1; 12)

Il y a un fax?

Is there a fax machine?

Anne comes down from her room to the reception desk. What does she ask for? Can you spot the two different formulations that Anne uses to ask about the hotel's facilities?

ANNE:	Excusez-moi, monsieur. Je voudrais envoyer un document. Vous avez un fax?
RECEPTIONNISTE:	Il y a un fax au premier étage, madame.
ANNE:	Ah, très bien. Il y a une piscine aussi, dans l'hôtel, non?
RECEPTIONNISTE:	Mais oui, madame. Nous avons une piscine et un sauna, au sous-sol. Il y a également une petite salle de gym.
ANNE:	Parfait. Et pour le petit déjeuner, c'est où?

RECEPTIONNISTE: C'est dans la salle de restaurant, au rez-de-chaussée, à côté de l'ascenseur. Il y a aussi un bar, juste à côté. Le petit déjeuner est servi entre 7 heures et 9 heures 30, madame.

ANNE: Je vous remercie, monsieur.

ANNE: *Excuse me. I would like to send a document. Do you have a fax machine?*

RECEPTIONIST: *There's a fax machine on the first floor.*

ANNE: *Oh, that's good. There's also a swimming pool in the hotel, isn't there?*

RECEPTIONIST: *Yes, madam. We have a swimming pool and a sauna, in the basement. There's also a small gym.*

ANNE: *Perfect. And where is breakfast served?*

RECEPTIONIST: *It's in the restaurant, on the ground floor, next to the lift. There's also a bar, just next to it. Breakfast is served between 7 and 9.30.*

ANNE: *Thank you.*

Language points

Did you notice?

un document	**une piscine**
un sauna	**une salle de gym**
le petit déjeuner	**la salle de restaurant**

All nouns in French are either masculine or feminine. Few nouns in English have a gender (e.g. man/woman, brother/sister) and English speakers might find it difficult to believe that **chaise** (chair) in French is feminine but **stylo** (pen) is masculine. There is no hard-and-fast rule. So, you will need to memorise the gender of a noun together with its meaning.

The gender of a noun will affect words directly connected with it (such as articles **un/une**, **le/la**) and their form will usually change accordingly. **Un/une** is usually the equivalent of *a/an* and **le/la** is usually the equivalent of *the*.

Nous avons *un* sauna.	**Nous avons *une* piscine.**
***Le* sauna est au sous-sol.**	***La* piscine est au sous-sol.**

Articles

Masculine	Feminine
un	**une**
le	**la**

Note that **le** and **la** become **l'** in front of a noun starting with a vowel or an **h**:

l'hôtel
l'ascenseur (the lift)

Exercise 1

Read the dialogue again. What is the gender of **fax** and **bar**? How can you tell?

Now, imagine you are the hotel manager explaining the facilities of your hotel to a customer.

Nous avons _____ (1) salle de gym _____ (2) restaurant _____ (3) bar et _____ (4) salon de coiffure (hair salon: m.).

_____ (5) salle de gym est au sous-sol. _____ (6) restaurant et _____ (7) bar sont au rez-de-chaussée. _____ (8) salon de coiffure est au deuxième étage.

Language points

Asking for information

You can ask for information with **il y a**. **Il y a** means 'there is' or 'there are'.

Il y a **une piscine?**
Is there a swimming pool?

Oui, *il y a* **une piscine au sixième étage.**
Yes, there is a swimming pool on the sixth floor.

You can also use **vous avez**.

Vous avez **un sauna?**
Do you have a sauna?

Oui, *nous avons* **un sauna.**
Yes, we have a sauna.

The verb avoir (to have)

J'**ai** un problème.	I have a problem.
Tu **as** un passeport?	Do you have a passport?
Il **a** un travail intéressant.	He has an interesting job.
Elle **a** une maison à Paris.	She has a house in Paris.
Nous **avons** deux enfants.	We have two children.
Vous **avez** un chat?	Do you have a cat?
Ils **ont** une voiture de sport.	They have a sports car.
Elles **ont** un restaurant.	They have a restaurant.

Exercise 2 (Audio 1; 13)

Imagine you are a customer in a hotel and ask for the following amenities. Use both **il y a** and **vous avez**.

piscine   bar
restaurant   fax
sauna   salon de coiffure

Language points

In a building

Look at the following:

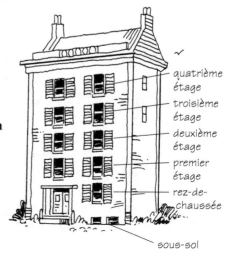

La chambre d'Anne Murdoch est *au premier étage.*
Anne Murdoch's room is on the first floor.

Le restaurant, c'est où?
C'est *au rez-de-chaussée.*
Where is the restaurant?
It's on the ground floor.

quatrième étage
troisième étage
deuxième étage
premier étage
rez-de-chaussée
sous-sol

Exercise 3 🎧 (Audio 1; 14)

Here is a table telling you where the facilities in a hotel are located.
Look at the table below and answer the questions as in the example.

> *Example*:   **Le salon de coiffure, c'est où?**
> **C'est au troisième étage.**
>
> *or*   **Vous avez un salon de coiffure?**
> **Oui, le salon de coiffure est au troisième étage.**

Troisième étage	Salon de coiffure
Deuxième étage	Fax-salle de conférence
Premier étage	Salle de gym
Rez-de-chaussée	Bar-restaurant
Sous-sol	Parking

1 Vous avez un fax?
2 La salle de conférence, c'est où?
3 Vous avez une salle de gym?
4 Et le bar, c'est où?
5 Vous avez un restaurant?
6 Et le parking, c'est où?

Dialogue 2 🎧 (Audio 1; 15)

Pour aller à l'Office du Tourisme, s'il vous plaît?

Can you tell me the way to the Tourist Information Office, please?

The following morning Anne asks the receptionist for facilities available in the town. Look at the map on p. 29 and try to understand the instructions given to her.

ANNE:	Bonjour monsieur. Je voudrais retirer de l'argent. Il y a un distributeur de billets, pas loin d'ici?
RECEPTIONNISTE:	Eh bien, vous avez une banque à 600 mètres. En sortant de l'hôtel, vous allez à gauche. Vous continuez tout droit et puis vous prenez la deuxième rue à droite. La banque est juste après le théâtre municipal.
ANNE:	Et pour aller à l'Office du Tourisme, c'est loin?
RECEPTIONNISTE:	Non, à 10 minutes à pied, madame. C'est dans le centre-ville. Attendez. Voilà le plan de la ville. Nous sommes ici. L'Office du Tourisme est là, vous voyez?
ANNE:	Et la banque, ici?
RECEPTIONNISTE:	Oui, c'est ça.
ANNE:	Merci monsieur.
RECEPTIONNISTE:	Je vous en prie, madame.

ANNE:	*Good morning. I would like to get some money. Is there a cash machine near here?*
RECEPTIONIST:	*There's a bank 600 metres from here. As you go out of the hotel, turn left. You carry straight on*

and then you take the second street on your right.
The bank is just past the theatre.

ANNE: What about the Tourist Information Office? Is it far?

RECEPTIONIST: No, ten minutes' walk. It's in the city centre. Wait. Here's the street plan. We are here. The Tourist Information Office is there, you see?

ANNE: And the bank, here?

RECEPTIONIST: Yes, that's right.

ANNE: Thank you.

RECEPTIONIST: You're welcome.

Language points

Asking for directions

To ask for directions, you can simply use **pour aller à** (literally *to go to*) in the following way:

Pour aller à l'Office du Tourisme, s'il vous plaît?
Can you tell me the way to the Tourist Information Office, please?

Pour aller à la poste, s'il vous plaît?
Pour aller à l'hôtel du Parc, s'il vous plaît?

When the noun following **pour aller à** is masculine and starts with a consonant, **à** and **le** combine to give **au**:

Pour aller au théâtre, s'il vous plaît?

Or, you can use **chercher** in the following way, particularly when you stop people in the street:

Excusez-moi, *je cherche* **une banque.**
Excuse me, I am looking for a bank.

Excusez-moi, *je cherche* **la gare.**
Excuse me, I am looking for the station.

Exercise 4

Using the expressions you have just learned, try asking the way to the places on the street plan.

Example: **Excusez-moi, je cherche la mairie, s'il vous plaît.**

   or   **Excusez-moi, pour aller à la mairie, s'il vous plaît?**

la mairie   the town hall
la pharmacie   the chemist's
la piscine   the swimming pool

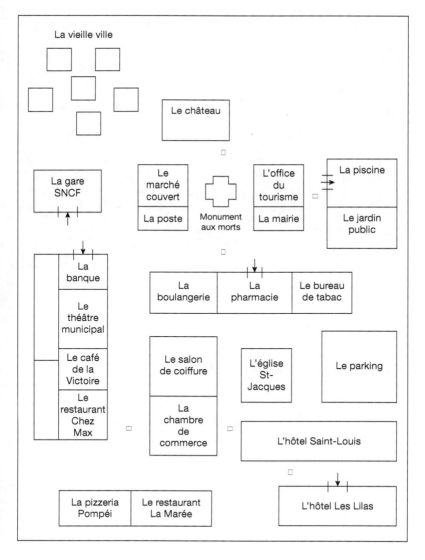

la poste	the post office
le château	the castle
la boulangerie	the bakery
le jardin public	the public garden
le marché couvert	the indoor market
la gare SNCF	the railway station

Language points

Counting from 60 to 1000 (Audio 1; 16)

For now, you only need to learn the following numbers. You can look at the reference grammar for further information.

60	**soixante**	200	**deux cents**
70	**soixante-dix**	250	**deux cent cinquante**
80	**quatre-vingts**	300	**trois cents**
90	**quatre-vingt-dix**	400	**quatre cents**
100	**cent**	500	**cinq cents**
150	**cent cinquante**	1000	**mille**

Asking for and giving directions

L'Office du Tourisme, c'est loin?
The Tourist Information Office, is it far?

Non, c'est à dix minutes à pied.
No, it's ten minutes' walk.

C'est à vingt minutes en voiture.
It's twenty minutes by car.

C'est à 600 mètres.
It's 600 metres (from here).

Exercise 5

Look at the drawing, showing the distances to some useful places.
Following the example, say how far these places are.

> *Example*: **La poste, c'est loin?**
> **Non, c'est à 100 mètres.**

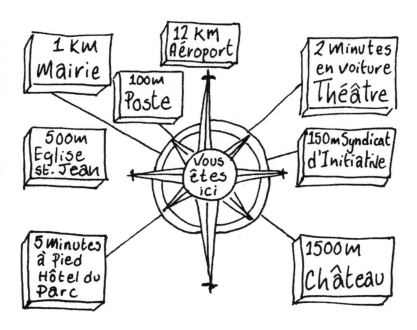

Language points

Giving more precise directions

You can give more precise directions by using the following expressions.

Vous allez	**à gauche**	You go	left
	à droite		right
	tout droit		straight on

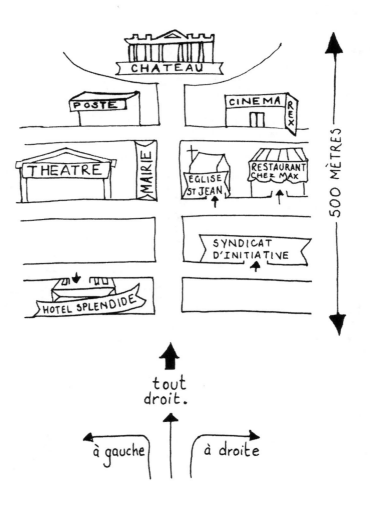

Vous continuez tout droit.   You carry straight on.

Vous tournez à gauche   You turn left
**   à droite**   right

Vous prenez la première rue à gauche.
You take   the first street on the left.

la deuxième rue à droite.
the second street on the right.

le boulevard Leclerc.
boulevard Leclerc.

Exercise 6

Do you remember where the bank is? Look at the map on p. 29
and fill in the blanks with the missing words.

Pour aller à la banque, en sortant de l'hôtel Les Lilas, vous
(1) _____ à gauche et vous (2) _____ tout droit. Vous
(3) _____ la deuxième rue à droite. La banque (4) _____
après le théâtre municipal.

What about these other locations?

Pour aller à la gare SNCF, en sortant de l'hôtel, vous allez
(5) _____ . Et puis vous prenez (6) _____ . Vous
continuez (7) _____ . Ensuite, vous tournez (8) _____ .
La gare SNCF est (9) _____.

Pour aller à la piscine, en sortant de la banque, vous (10)
_____ et vous (11) _____ tout droit. Après la mairie,
vous (12) _____ à gauche. La piscine (13) _____ à
droite.

Exercise 7 🎧 (Audio 1; 17)

You have just come out of the restaurant **La Marée** and are
intending to visit the **château**. You are walking up the street and
are level with the **café de la Victoire**. A couple of people ask you
for directions. Look at the map on p. 29 and direct them.

1 Excusez-moi, je cherche une pharmacie.
2 Excusez-moi, pour aller à la gare, s'il vous plaît?

Exercise 8

Look at the plan on p. 29 and complete it by naming the square and streets.

1 La poste est sur la place de la Libération.
2 En sortant de l'hôtel, vous êtes sur le boulevard Saint-Denis.
3 Le restaurant Chez Max, le théâtre municipal et la chambre de commerce sont sur l'avenue du 11 Novembre.
4 La mairie et la pharmacie sont situées sur le cours Pasteur.
5 Pour aller à l'église Saint-Jacques, en sortant de l'hôtel Les Lilas, vous tournez à droite dans la rue du Temple.
6 Il y a une piscine et un jardin public sur l'allée des Tilleuls.

Both **un cours** and **une allée** or **des allées** tend to be broader avenues. **La place** (the town square), when you hear it in the context of a small town, will refer to the main town square and will often, if not always, have **un monument aux morts**, a monument to commemorate the people who died during the First and Second World Wars. **La Libération** refers to the liberation in the Second World War and **le 11 novembre** is the date of the armistice at the end of the First World War.

3 Manger et boire

Eating and drinking

In this unit, you will learn about:

- how to order food and drinks
- how to express your likes and dislikes
- how to ask for explanations about dishes
- **moi, toi, lui** . . .
- **tu** and **vous**
- the plural of nouns and the articles **des** and **les**

Dialogue 1 (Audio 1; 18)

Déjeuner entre amis

Lunch with friends

Anne Murdoch has lunch in a brasserie *with a couple of French friends. They opt for a fixed menu,* menu à 25 euros *rather than the more expensive lunch* à la carte.

ANNE: Juliette, qu'est-ce que c'est, un carpaccio de saumon?
JULIETTE: C'est des tranches fines de saumon cru, je crois.
FRANÇOIS: Oui, c'est ça. Dis, l'assiette printanière, c'est bien des légumes?
JULIETTE: Oui, c'est excellent! Il y a des asperges, des tomates, des artichauts frais. . .
FRANÇOIS: Mmm, j'adore les artichauts et les asperges!
ANNE: J'hésite entre l'assiette printanière et les moules. . . J'aime bien les moules.

JULIETTE: Moi, je déteste les moules. Remarquez, je n'aime pas
              beaucoup le poisson, sauf le thon.
ANNE: Le steak tartare, c'est cru, non?
FRANÇOIS: Oui, c'est un steak haché avec un jaune d'œuf cru et
              des herbes.
ANNE: Bon, je prends l'escalope de veau à la crème et
              l'assiette printanière en entrée.
JULIETTE: Et moi, un bon fondant au chocolat en dessert!
FRANÇOIS: Tu ne changes pas, toi! Tu choisis toujours le dessert
              en premier!

ANNE: *Juliette, what is a carpaccio of salmon?*
JULIETTE: *It's thin slices of raw salmon, I think.*
FRANÇOIS: *Yes, that's it. The* assiette printanière *is vegetables,
              isn't it?*
JULIETTE: *Yes, it's excellent. There's asparagus, tomatoes, fresh
              artichokes. . .*

❧ Brasserie le Galion ☙

Menu à 25 euros

Carpaccio de saumon
Assiette printanière
Soupe de poisson
Moules marinière

―◦―

Truite aux amandes
Thon grillé
Steak tartare
Escalope de veau à la crème

―◦―

Assiette de fromages
ou
Desserts

Tarte aux pommes
Glaces et sorbets
Fondant au chocolat

FRANÇOIS:	*Mm, I love artichokes and asparagus!*
ANNE:	*I can't decide between the* assiette printanière *and the mussels . . . I quite like mussels.*
JULIETTE:	*I hate mussels. Mind you, I don't like fish very much apart from tuna.*
ANNE:	*Steak tartare, it's raw, isn't it?*
FRANÇOIS:	*Yes, it's a minced steak with a raw egg yolk and herbs.*
ANNE:	*Well, I'll have the veal escalope with cream and the* assiette printanière *as a starter.*
JULIETTE:	*And I'll have a lovely chocolate fondant for dessert!*
FRANÇOIS:	*You'll never change. You always choose the dessert first!*

Language points

Did you notice?

des **légumes**	vegetables
des **tomates**	tomatoes
des **artichauts**	artichokes
des **herbes**	herbs
les **moules**	mussels
les **asperges**	asparagus
les **artichauts**	artichokes

Though there are exceptions (some are given in the reference grammar), nouns in the plural usually end with '**s**'.

Un and **une** become **des** in the plural and **le**, **la** and **l'** become **les**.

Articles

Masculine	Feminine	Plural
un	**une**	**des**
le/l'	**la/l'**	**les**

Remember that, most of the time and unlike in English, French requires an article in front of the noun.

Vous avez *des* amis?	Do you have friends?
J'adore *les* tomates.	I love tomatoes.

Exercise 1

Can you spot the other nouns in the plural in the dialogue and the menu?

The waiter is explaining to Anne what the **salade printanière** consists of. Complete the sentence with the ingredients given below.

Dans la salade printanière, il y a des artichauts ...

tomate	asperge
oignon	carotte

Language points

Saying what you like and don't like
(Audio 1; 19)

To enquire about what someone likes, you can use the following questions:

Vous aimez **le poisson?**
Do you like fish?

Qu'est-ce que **vous aimez?**
What do you like?

To answer the previous questions, you can use the following verbs: **aimer**, **adorer**, **détester**. They all follow the pattern of **travailler**. **Aimer** is often used in combination with **beaucoup**, **bien** to express how much you like something. **Ne ... pas beaucoup**, **ne ... pas tellement** and **ne ... pas du tout** are also used very frequently with this verb.

♥♥♥   **J'***adore* **la mousse au chocolat.**
       I love chocolate mousse.

♥♥   **J'***aime beaucoup* **les légumes.**
       I like vegetables a lot.

♥   **J'***aime bien* **les fruits.**
       I quite like fruit.

♠   **Je** *n'aime pas beaucoup/tellement* **les escargots.**
       I am not too keen on snails.

♠♠　　**Je *n'aime pas du tout* le poulet.**
　　　I don't like chicken at all.

♠♠♠　　**Je *déteste* les épinards.**
　　　I hate spinach.

Remember that you will need **le**, **la**, **l'** or **les** in front of the noun.

Il est végétarien parce qu'il n'*aime* pas du tout *la* viande.
He is a vegetarian because he does not like meat at all.

Exercice 2

Read Dialogue 1 again and say if the following statements are true or false (**vrai ou faux**). Whenever they are not true, correct them by giving the right statement.

> *Example*: **François n'aime pas les artichauts et les asperges.**
> **C'est faux. François adore les artichauts et les asperges.**

1　Anne aime bien les moules.
2　Juliette adore les moules.
3　Juliette aime beaucoup le poisson.
4　Juliette n'aime pas du tout les desserts.

Exercice 3 🎧 (Audio 1; 20)

Look at the list of food and drinks below and using the previous examples as a model, make sentences to say what you like or do not like.

le chocolat	le poisson	les tomates
les épinards	le cognac	les glaces
les huîtres (oysters)		

Language points

Expressing preferences

You can use the verb **préférer** to say you prefer something:

Qu'est-ce que vous préférez?
What do you prefer?

J'aime bien les moules mais je *préfère* les huîtres.
I quite like mussels but I prefer oysters.

Anne hesitates between the mussels and the **assiette printanière**.
She has not made up her mind yet as to what dish she would prefer.

Anne *hésite entre* les moules et l'assiette printanière.

Exercise 4 (Audio 1; 21)

Qu'est-ce que vous préférez? For each two items of food below,
using the verbs you have learned, say that you like one but prefer
the other.

1 snails, oysters   3 chicken, fish
2 ice cream, apple pie   4 steak tartare, tuna

Language points

Did you notice?

Anne did not know what a **carpaccio de saumon** was. So she asked
Juliette:

> *Qu'est-ce que c'est,* **un carpaccio de saumon?**
> (literally) What is it, a carpaccio of salmon?

> *C'est* **des tranches fines de saumon cru.**
> (literally) It's thin slices of raw salmon.

Because **tranches** is plural, strictly speaking, Juliette should have
said:

> *Ce sont* **des tranches fines de saumon cru.**

But increasingly, and especially in the spoken language, the French
will use **c'est** even if the noun that follows is in the plural.

Exercise 5

Using **qu'est-ce que c'est**, ask what the following are:

1 une assiette de crudités
2 un carpaccio de bœuf
3 le Ricard®
4 une assiette de charcuterie

Now match what you think the above are with the short descriptions below:

(a) un alcool au parfum d'anis
(b) des tranches fines de bœuf cru
(c) des tranches de charcuterie: saucisson, jambon, pâté ...
(d) une sélection de légumes crus: tomates, carottes, céleri ...

And then answer the questions:

(i) Qu'est-ce que c'est, une assiette de crudités?
(ii) Qu'est-ce que c'est, un carpaccio de bœuf?
(iii) Qu'est-ce que c'est, le Ricard®?
(iv) Qu'est-ce que c'est, une assiette de charcuterie?

Dialogue 2 (Audio 1; 22)

Au café

In the café

Later in the day, Anne and her friends stop at a café for a drink.

ANNE: Oh, là, là, quelle chaleur! J'ai soif et je suis crevée!
SERVEUR: Messieurs-dames, vous avez choisi? Qu'est-ce que
           je vous sers?

ANNE: Je voudrais un Perrier® menthe, s'il vous plaît.
JULIETTE: Moi, je prends un Coca® light.
SERVEUR: Avec des glaçons, mesdames?
ANNE & JULIETTE: Oui, oui.
SERVEUR: Et vous, monsieur, qu'est-ce que vous prenez?
FRANÇOIS: Pour moi, une bière pression, s'il vous plaît. Vous
                avez de la Kronenbourg®?
SERVEUR: Oui, bien sûr. Un demi?
FRANÇOIS: Oui, s'il vous plaît.
SERVEUR: Alors, un demi, un Perrier® menthe et un Coca®
                light.
FRANÇOIS: Tu ne prends pas une petite pâtisserie, Juliette?
JULIETTE: Non, je n'ai pas faim.

ANNE: *Oh, it's really hot! I'm thirsty and I'm knackered!*
WAITER: *Have you chosen? What would you like?*
ANNE: *I would like a Perrier® menthe, please.*
JULIETTE: *I'll have a Diet Coke®.*
WAITER: *With ice?*
ANNE & JULIETTE: *Yes.*
WAITER: *What about you, sir? What are you having?*
FRANÇOIS: *A (draught) beer please. Do you have Kronen-*
                bourg®?
WAITER: *Yes, of course. A half?*
FRANÇOIS: *Yes, please.*
WAITER: *So, a half of lager, a Perrier® menthe and a Diet*
                Coke®.
FRANÇOIS: *Are you going to have a little cake, Juliette?*
JULIETTE: *No, I'm not hungry.*

Language points

Ordering food and drinks

In a restaurant or a café, you are likely to hear the waiter say to
you:

Vous avez choisi?
(literally) Have you chosen?

Qu'est-ce que vous prenez?
What are you having?

Qu'est-ce que je vous sers?
(literally) What am I serving you?

You can reply in the following ways:

Je *voudrais* une bière.
I would like a beer.

Je *prends* un café.
I'll have a coffee.

Un thé, s'il vous plaît.
A tea, please.

The verb prendre **(to take)**

Je **prends** un Coca®

Tu **prends** une glace

Il **prend** un café

Elle **prend** un dessert

Nous **prenons** une bouteille de vin

Vous **prenez** un chocolat

Ils **prennent** un taxi

Elles **prennent** le bus

Here are a few popular drinks (**des boissons**) which the French like to have when they go to a café:

une eau minérale gazeuse   **une eau minérale non gazeuse**
sparkling mineral water   still mineral water

Note that the French will normally ask for a specific brand.

Vocabulary

une menthe à l'eau	a sort of mint-flavoured cordial (**sirop**) with a distinctive green colour, diluted with water
un demi	a half of lager
un demi-panaché	a half of lager-shandy
un jus d'orange	orange juice
un jus de pamplemousse	grapefruit juice
un jus de tomate	tomato juice
un café	a coffee
un café crème	coffee with hot milk
un thé au lait	tea with milk
un thé au citron	tea with a slice of lemon
un kir	a glass of dry white wine with a dash of blackcurrant syrup

Cultural point

There are other drinks of course. Bear in mind that most French people do not go to a café to drink alcohol. They will enjoy **un apéritif** in the early evening and will move on fairly rapidly to have a meal. **Le vin** (wine) is not normally drunk outside meals or **apéritifs**. And if, like many French, you go to a café to enjoy **un café**, remember that you will be served an espresso!

Exercise 6 🎧 (Audio 1; 23)

Fill in the blanks with the correct forms of **prendre** in the following dialogue.

SERVEUR:	Messieurs-dames, qu'est-ce que vous (1) _____ ?
SYLVIE:	Je (2) _____ un Orangina® s'il vous plaît.
PIERRE:	Tu ne (3) _____ pas un demi?
SYLVIE:	Non, je n'aime pas tellement la bière.
PIERRE:	Et toi, Mary, qu'est-ce que tu (4) _____ ?
MARY:	Qu'est-ce qu'ils (5) _____ à la table à côté?
SERVEUR:	Une menthe à l'eau, madame.

Here is the rest of the dialogue. Mary's part has been cut out: work out what she says.

MARY: (6) _____ .
PIERRE: C'est un sirop de menthe avec de l'eau.
MARY: (7) _____ .
PIERRE: Moi aussi!
SERVEUR: Alors, deux menthes à l'eau et un Orangina®.

Language points

Did you notice?

Moi, je **prends un Coca® light.**
I am having a Diet Coke®.

Et toi **Mary, qu'est-ce que** *tu* **prends?**
What about you Mary? What are you having?

Pour moi, **une bière pression, s'il vous plaît.**
A (draught) beer for me, please.

Alongside the forms of the pronouns **je**, **tu**, **il**, **elle**, etc., the French language also has the strong forms **moi**, **toi**, **lui**, **elle** as follows.

je	*moi*	nous	*nous*
tu	*toi*	vous	*vous*
il	*lui*	ils	*eux*
elle	*elle*	elles	*elles*

You will need to use these strong forms:

• when you want to put some **emphasis** on the person (**je**, **tu**, **il**, **elle**, etc.):

   Moi, je **prends une bière**;

• after **c'est**:

   C'est *Pierre*?   **Oui, c'est** *lui.*
   Is it Pierre?   Yes it's him.

• after words such as **pour**, **avec** and **et**:

   Pour moi, **un Coca®.**   **Il est** *avec moi.*
   Et toi?   He is with me.

Language points

Using tu *and* vous

You may have noticed in Dialogue 2 how François addressed Juliette, using **tu**:

> *Tu* **ne prends pas une petite pâtisserie, Juliette?**

Vous can be used to address one person or more than one person whereas **tu** can only be used to address one person.

Tu is normally only used for members of a family, friends and young children. **Vous** is used whenever you do not know the person you are talking to very well or at all. As the French tend to be more formal than the British, they will use **vous** at work, especially with colleagues of a higher rank. If in doubt about what you should use when talking to a French-speaking person, use **vous** and wait until you are invited to use **tu**. The French normally use two verbs – **vouvoyer** (to use **vous**) and **tutoyer** (to use **tu**) – to indicate this.

Il me *tutoie.*	**Nous le** *vouvoyons.*
He uses *tu* with me.	We use *vous* with him.

Exercise 7

Put the words in the right speech bubbles.

Oui, et toi?	Vous travaillez à Londres?
Oui, et vous?	Tu prends un café?

1   2

Language points

Did you notice?

une soupe *de* poisson   une glace *à* la fraise
un jus *d'*orange   une truite *aux* amandes
    (aux = à + les)
une assiette *de* crudités   une tarte *aux* pommes
    (aux = à + les)

The French will normally link two nouns together with words such as **à** or **de**. Whereas **de** will indicate what a dish or drink is made of, **à** will refer to a flavour or particular way in which a dish or drink is prepared. This is a subtle difference and even the French are not too sure which one they should use sometimes! So, don't worry. You will learn more about **à** and **de** in Unit 4.

Exercise 8

Fill in the blanks with **à, aux, de**, or **d'**:

1 Une menthe ___ l'eau
2 Une glace ___ la vanille
3 Une tarte ___ abricots
4 Un jus ___ ananas (pineapple juice)
5 Un civet ___ lapin (rabbit stew)

4 Rencontres

Meeting people

In this unit you will learn about:

- introducing yourself
- telling people about yourself
- talking about your hobbies
- **aller**, **jouer** and **faire**
- **aimer**, **adorer**, **détester** + verb in the infinitive

Dialogue 1 ⌒ (Audio 1; 25)

Faire connaissance (1)

Getting to know people

At the bar of the hotel, Anne Murdoch meets a French couple in their fifties on holiday. Focus on how they talk about their occupations.

ANNE:	Excusez-moi, cette chaise est libre?
JACQUES:	Mais oui, je vous en prie. Il y a beaucoup de monde, ce soir.
ANNE:	Oui, c'est surprenant!
CHANTAL:	Vous êtes anglaise?
ANNE:	Non, je suis écossaise.
JACQUES:	Ah bon, vous venez de loin, alors.
ANNE:	De Glasgow. Mais, en fait, j'habite à Coventry. Et vous? Vous venez d'où?
CHANTAL:	Nous sommes de Paris.
ANNE:	Ah Paris, quelle ville magnifique! Vous êtes en vacances?

CHANTAL: Moi, oui, je suis retraitée, mais mon mari est ici pour le travail.

JACQUES: Je suis représentant pour une société informatique. Et vous? Qu'est-ce que vous faites dans la vie?

ANNE: Je travaille dans l'industrie. Je suis comptable. Mais, en ce moment, je suis en vacances et comme j'adore la France . . .

CHANTAL: Vous avez bien raison!

ANNE: *Excuse me, is anybody sitting here? (literally: Is this chair free?)*

JACQUES: *No, please take it. It's very busy tonight. (literally: There are a lot of people)*

ANNE: *Yes, it's surprising.*

CHANTAL: *Are you English?*

ANNE: *No I'm Scottish.*

JACQUES: *So you have come a long way.*

ANNE: *From Glasgow. But I actually live in Coventry. What about you? Where are you from?*

CHANTAL: *We are from Paris.*

ANNE: *Ah, Paris, what a beautiful city! Are you on holiday?*

CHANTAL: *I am. I'm retired, but my husband is here for work.*

JACQUES: *I'm a rep for an IT company. What about you? What do you do?*

ANNE: *I'm in industry. I'm an accountant. But at the moment, I'm on holiday and as I love France. . .*

CHANTAL: *And you're so right!*

Language points

Telling people about yourself (1)

To ask about someone's occupation, you can use the following phrases:

Qu'est-ce que vous faites dans la vie?
(literally) What do you do in life?

Vous êtes professeur?	Are you a teacher?
comptable?	an accountant?
médecin?	a doctor?

Quelle est votre profession?
Quel est votre métier?
Both: What is your job?

You can answer these questions like this:

Je travaille dans une entreprise d'informatique.
I work in an IT company.

Je travaille dans une banque.
I work in a bank.

Il travaille dans le marketing.
He works/is in marketing.

Elle travaille dans le journalisme.
She works/is in journalism.

You can also use:

Je suis + your occupation

Je suis	**journaliste.**
	chauffeur de taxi.
	fonctionnaire. (a Civil Servant)

Some occupations also have a feminine form:

Il est	**mécanicien.**	He is a mechanic.
Elle est	**mécanicienne.**	She is a mechanic.
Il est	**serveur.**	He is a waiter.
Elle est	**serveuse.**	She is a waitress.
Il est	**étudiant.**	He is a student.
Elle est	**étudiante.**	She is a student.

Here are some more:

vendeur	**vendeuse**	salesman/ -woman
chanteur	**chanteuse**	singer
coiffeur	**coiffeuse**	hairdresser
acteur	**actrice**	actor/actress
infirmier	**infirmière**	nurse
employé de banque	**employée de banque**	bank clerk
facteur	**factrice**	postman/ -woman

Did you notice that, unlike in English, in French you do not need the article *a/an* when you say what you do:

Je suis architecte. I am an architect.

Exercise 1

What do these people do? Choose their correct occupation from the box below.

1 Marie travaille dans un hôpital.
   Elle est _____ .

2 Pierre travaille dans un grand restaurant.
   Il est _____ .

3 Ivan et Samia travaillent dans une banque.
   _____ .

4 Juliette travaille dans un cabaret parisien.
   _____ .

5 Ahmed travaille pour un journal.
   _____ .

6 Nathalie ne travaille pas. Elle est encore dans les études.
   _____ .

> chef cuisinier   chanteur   chanteuse
> infirmière   ingénieur   journaliste
> infirmier   vendeur   factrice   étudiante
> employés de banque

Dialogue 2 (Audio 1; 27)

Faire connaissance (2)

Getting to know people

Anne and the couple talk about more personal information. Focus on how they introduce themselves and talk about their family status.

ANNE:	Vous êtes ici pour quelques jours?
CHANTAL:	Oui, deux ou trois. Puis, nous allons à Limoges pour passer une semaine chez notre fils.
ANNE:	Ah, vous avez des enfants?
JACQUES:	Oui, deux. Charles, qui habite à Limoges, et Christine.
ANNE:	Ils ont quel âge?
CHANTAL:	Charles a trente ans. Il est ingénieur. Et Christine a vingt-quatre ans. Elle est encore étudiante en médecine. Et vous, vous êtes mariée? Vous avez des enfants?
ANNE:	Non, je suis célibataire et je n'ai pas d'enfants. C'est peut-être le moment de me présenter. Je m'appelle Anne.
JACQUES:	Moi, c'est Jacques. Enchanté.
CHANTAL:	Et moi, je m'appelle Chantal. Ravie de faire votre connaissance, Anne.

ANNE:	*Are you here for a few days?*
CHANTAL:	*Yes, two or three. Then we're going to Limoges to spend a week at our son's.*
ANNE:	*So, you have children?*
JACQUES:	*Yes, two. Charles who lives in Limoges, and Christine.*
ANNE:	*How old are they?*
CHANTAL:	*Charles is 30. He is an engineer. And Christine is 24. She is still a medical student. What about you? Are you married? Do you have children?*
ANNE:	*No, I'm single and I don't have children. Maybe, it's time to introduce myself. I'm Anne.*
JACQUES:	*I'm Jacques. Pleased to meet you.*
CHANTAL:	*I'm Chantal. Delighted to meet you, Anne.*

Language points

Telling people about yourself (2)

The following can be used:

Je m'appelle + your name
Moi, c'est + your name

In more formal situations, such as in business settings, you might say:

Je suis + your name

Notice how Jacques and Chantal respond to Anne's introduction with:

Enchanté
Ravie de faire votre connaissance

To talk about your status, you use **être** and say:

Je suis célibataire.	**Vous êtes marié?**
I am single.	Are you married?
Il est retraité.	**Nous sommes divorcés.**
He is retired.	We are divorced.

Did you notice?

As with nationalities, **ravi**, **enchanté**, **retraité**, **divorcé** and **marié** will have an 'e' if the person concerned is a woman, and an 's' if more than one person is concerned.

Exercise 2 (Audio 1; 28)

Answer the following questions.

1 Anne est mariée?
Elle n'est _____ . Elle est _____ .

2 Jacques et Chantal sont divorcés?
Ils ne sont _____ . Ils sont _____ .

3 Jacques est retraité?
Il _____ .

4 Et vous? Vous êtes marié(e)?
Je suis _____ .

Language points

In French, when you talk about your age, you use **avoir**:

Vous avez quel âge?
How old are you?

J'ai vingt-quatre ans.
I am 24 (years old).

You can also use **avoir** to say how many children you have:

J'ai deux enfants.   **Je n'ai pas d'enfants.**
I have two chidren.   I have no children.

Exercise 3

Answer the following questions.

1 Charles a quel âge?   _____
2 Et Christine? Elle a quel âge?   _____
3 Et vous?   _____

Exercise 4

In French, the name Claude can be given to a man or a woman. In the following example, can you tell whether Claude is a man or a woman? How?

Match the correct question to the appropriate answer.

1 J'ai trois enfants.   (a) Vous êtes mariée?
2 Je suis française.   (b) Vous avez quel âge?
3 Non, je ne suis pas mariée.   (c) Vous avez des enfants?
4 Je m'appelle Claude.   (d) Quelle est votre nationalité?
5 J'ai quarante ans.   (e) Vous vous appelez
                                     comment?

Exercise 5 (Audio 1; 29)

Look at the two descriptions of Christian and Daniella and write out in full sentences what you know about them.

Christian Dufresne

Nationalité française

54 ans

marié

2 enfants: Natasha 28 ans,
Emilie 34 ans

profession: acteur

Daniella Cecaldi

Nationalité italienne

38 ans

célibataire

sans enfants

profession: directrice du
marketing

Dialogue 3 (Audio 1; 30)

Parler loisirs

Talking about leisure activities

Anne Murdoch and Chantal meet again the following afternoon while Jacques is working. Make a list of the activities Anne, Chantal and Jacques do and pay attention to the new verbs.

ANNE: Vous êtes retraitée. Vous ne vous ennuyez pas?
CHANTAL: Oh non. Je suis très sportive. Je joue au golf. Et puis,
           j'aime bien marcher et faire du vélo.
ANNE: Et votre mari, il est sportif aussi?

CHANTAL: Pas du tout. Il n'aime pas beaucoup le sport, sauf à
             la télévision! Surtout les matches de rugby et de foot-
             ball! Mais, il est actif, quand même. Il va à la pêche
             le dimanche et il joue aux échecs dans un petit club.
ANNE: Vous êtes très différents alors?
CHANTAL: Ça, oui! Il travaille beaucoup. Il n'a pas vraiment de
             temps pour les loisirs. Quelquefois, nous faisons du
             tennis ou du vélo ensemble, mais c'est rare. Et vous?
             Qu'est-ce que vous faites de votre temps libre?
ANNE: Moi aussi, comme votre mari, je déteste faire de
             l'exercice. Je préfère lire ou aller au concert. J'adore
             la musique, surtout le jazz. Mais pour rester en forme,
             je vais quand même à la piscine une ou deux fois par
             semaine avec une amie.

ANNE: *You are retired. Don't you get bored?*
CHANTAL: *Oh no! I'm very sporty. I play golf. And I like walking
             and cycling.*
ANNE: *And is your husband fond of sport, too?*
CHANTAL: *Not at all. He doesn't like sport very much, except on
             TV! Especially rugby and football matches! But still,
             he is active. He goes fishing on Sundays and he plays
             chess in a small club.*
ANNE: *You are very different, then?*
CHANTAL: *You can say that again! He works a lot. He doesn't
             really have much time for leisure activities. Sometimes,
             we play tennis or cycle together, but rarely. What about
             you? What do you do with your free time?*
ANNE: *Like your husband, I hate exercise, too. I prefer
             reading or going to a concert. I love music, especially
             jazz. But, to keep fit, I do go swimming once or twice
             a week with a friend.*

Language points

Talking about leisure

To start a conversation on this topic, you could begin with:

Qu'est-ce que vous faites de votre temps libre?
How do you spend your free time?

To talk about things you do, you can use two verbs: **aller** and **faire**.

Je vais au cinéma.
I go to the cinema.

Elle va à l'école.
She goes to school.

Je fais du tennis.
I play tennis.

Il fait de l'exercice.
He exercises.

The verbs aller (to go) and faire (to do or to make)

Je **vais** à la piscine.

Tu **vas** au cinéma?

Il **va** au match de football.

Elle **va** au restaurant.

Nous **allons** au cinéma.

Vous **allez** au théâtre?

Ils **vont** aux toilettes.

Elles **vont** à l'hôtel.

Je **fais** du tennis.

Tu **fais** du sport?

Il **fait** de la moto.

Elle **fait** du sport.

Nous **faisons** du football.

Vous **faites** du yoga?

Ils **font** de l'équitation.
(horse riding)

Elles **font** de l'escalade.
(climbing)

Did you notice that **aller** does not follow the pattern of the **-er** verbs (**aimer**, **parler**, **jouer**) we encountered in the previous chapters?

Exercise 6

Aller or **faire**?

1 Pierre _____ de l'exercice régulièrement.

2 Nous _____ souvent au cinéma.

3 Vous _____ au théâtre, ce soir?

4 Tu _____ un gâteau au chocolat?

5 Je _____ au match de rugby.

6 Cécile _____ du tennis.

7 Elles _____ du golf.

Language points

Did you notice?

à when used with **le** and **les**, combines to give **au** and **aux**.

Nous allons	*à la* **piscine**	**la piscine**	
	au **cinéma**	**le cinéma**	(**à** + **le** = **au**)
	*à l'*école	**l'école**	
	aux **toilettes**	**les toilettes**	(**à** + **les** = **aux**)

de when used with **le**, combines to give **du**.

Il fait	*de la* **voile**	**la voile**	(sailing)
	du **tennis**	**le tennis**	(**de** + **le** = **du**)
	*de l'*exercice	**l'exercice**	

Exercise 7

1 Using the words in the three columns, make up sentences.

Example: **Pierre fait du squash.**

Pierre	faisons	le jogging	
Nous	faites	la marche	(hiking)
Vous	fait	le squash	
Tu	fais	l'équitation	(horse riding)

2 Now repeat this with **aller**.

Marie et Chantal	vais	la piscine
Jacques	allez	l'hôpital
Je	va	le centre-ville
Vous	vont	les Etats-Unis (USA)

3 In the dialogue between Chantal and Anne, can you spot the verb used twice that uses the same construction as **aller à**?

Language points

Using another verb in the infinitive to talk about things you like to do

In previous lessons, you have used **aimer**, **adorer**, **détester** in this way:

J'aime *le poisson.*
Vous détestez *le sport?*
Il adore le *jambon de Parme.*

But you can also use these verbs with another verb in the infinitive:

J'aime *faire* **du sport.**
Vous détestez *manger* **au restaurant?**
Il adore *jouer* **au bridge.**

Read the dialogue again. Can you find examples to add to the list?

Exercise 8 🎧 (Audio 1; 32)

What do you like or dislike doing? Use **aimer**, **adorer**, **détester**.

Qu'est-ce que vous aimez ou détestez faire?

lire	(reading)
faire le ménage	(doing the housework)
regarder la télévision	(watching TV)
faire de l'exercice	(exercising)
faire la cuisine	(cooking)
partir en vacances	(going on holiday)

Exercise 9

Test your memory: Which of the following statements are correct? Correct any mistakes by rewriting the false statements.

1 Jacques est ingénieur.
2 Chantal et Jacques sont français et habitent à Limoges.
3 Anne est en vacances.
4 Chantal et Jacques ont deux fils.
5 Jacques est sportif mais Chantal déteste faire de l'exercice.
6 Anne adore le jazz.
7 Jacques n'aime pas aller à la pêche.

5 Projets de vacances

Holiday plans

In this unit you will learn about:

- talking about future projects
- using **on** and **nous**
- **savoir, connaître**
- using **en** and **au** with names of countries
- using **en** and **au** with months and seasons
- **partir, rentrer** with dates

Dialogue 1 🎧 (Audio 1; 33)

Projets de vacances

Holiday plans

Chantal and Jacques tell Anne about what they are going to do during the rest of their holiday. Can you find the two forms that they use to talk about what they are going to do?

ANNE:	Qu'est-ce que vous allez faire?
JACQUES:	Nous allons passer deux ou trois jours à Limoges avec notre fils et puis nous allons louer un petit studio en Provence pour une semaine.
CHANTAL:	Oui, je ne connais pas la Provence. On va visiter les monuments romains, les arènes de Nîmes, le pont du Gard ... Et vous, vous avez des projets?
ANNE:	Mes vacances sont presque finies, malheureusement, mais j'ai l'intention de louer une voiture pour le

week-end. En automne, je vais peut-être aller en Italie, avec une amie. Elle prend toujours des vacances en septembre. Et de là, on va probablement prendre le bateau pour la Sicile. Je ne connais pas la Sicile. Et vous?

CHANTAL: Moi non plus. Mais l'Italie est un pays magnifique, vous savez!

ANNE: *What are you going to do?*
JACQUES: *We are going to spend two or three days in Limoges with our son and then we are going to rent a small studio in Provence for a week.*
CHANTAL: *Ah, I don't know Provence. We are going to visit the Roman monuments; the amphitheatre in Nîmes, the pont du Gard ... What about you? Do you have plans?*
ANNE: *My holidays are nearly finished, unfortunately, although I intend to rent a car for the weekend. But in the autumn I might go to Italy with a friend. She always takes a holiday in September. And from there, we are probably going to take the boat to Sicily. I don't know Sicily. Do you?*
CHANTAL: *I don't either. But Italy is a wonderful country, you know!*

Le Pont du Gard

Language points

Talking about what you are going to do

Qu'est-ce que vous allez faire?
What are you going to do?

To talk about what you are going to do, you can use:

> **aller** in the **present** tense + any other **verb**
> in the **infinitive** form

Nous *allons passer* **deux ou trois jours à Limoges.**
Nous *allons louer* **un petit studio.**
Je *vais* **peut-être** *aller* **en Italie.**

When you want to use **ne ... pas** with this form, this is how to do it:

Je **ne** vais **pas** aller en France.
Elle **ne** va **pas** prendre de vacances.

Exercise 1

Read the dialogue again and fill in the gaps with the form you have just learned.

Jacques et Chantal (1) _____ deux ou trois jours à Limoges.
Ensuite, ils (2) _____ un petit studio en Provence.
Anne (3) _____ une voiture pour le week-end. En automne,
elle (4) _____ en Italie avec une amie. Elles (5) _____ le
bateau pour la Sicile.

Language points

Did you notice?

In the dialogue, we used another form to talk about future plans:

> **avoir l'intention de** + another **verb** in the **infinitive**

J'ai l'intention de louer une voiture pour le week-end.

Je *n'ai pas* l'intention de prendre des vacances
en septembre.

Exercise 2

True or false? **Vrai ou faux?** Correct the wrong statements by
putting them in the negative form, using **ne . . . pas**.

1 Jacques et Chantal vont aller à Limoges.

2 Ils vont louer un petit studio en Sicile.

3 Anne va passer deux ou trois jours à Limoges.

4 Anne va prendre des vacances en septembre.

5 Jacques et Chantal ont l'intention de louer une voiture pour
le week-end.

Language points

Saying where and when you are going

en is used with names of countries when they are feminine:

J'habite *en* Grèce.	(**la Grèce**)
Je travaille *en* France.	(**la France**)
Je vais *en* Italie.	(**l'Italie**)

au and **aux** are used with the masculine and the plural:

Elle va *au* Japon.	(**le Japon**)
Il habite *aux* Etats-Unis.	(**les Etats-Unis**: the United States)

Most of the time, you can also use **en** with names of regions:

Nous allons *en* Provence.
J'habite *en* Normandie.

You can also use **en** with the months of the year:

Je vais en Italie *en* septembre.

Les mois de l'année (months of the year)
(Audio 1; 35)

janvier	mai	septembre
février	juin	octobre
mars	juillet	novembre
avril	août	décembre

And with all seasons except **printemps**:

Nous allons passer six jours à Paris en automne.
We are going to spend six days in Paris in the autumn.

l'été summer	***en* été** in the summer	**l'automne** autumn	***en* automne** in the autumn
l'hiver winter	***en* hiver** in the winter	**le printemps** spring	***au* printemps** in the spring

Exercise 3

Fill in the gaps with the missing words (**en**, **au**, **à**, **aux**, **le**).

Pierre est toujours en vacances! Il va (1) _____ Espagne (2) _____ hiver, normalement (3) _____ décembre. (4) _____ printemps, il préfère aller (5) _____ Japon. Il adore (6) _____ printemps (7) _____ Japon. Il va passer deux ou trois jours (8) _____ Italie, (9) _____ juin. Et (10) _____ automne, il va souvent (11) _____ Etats-Unis, (12) _____ New York. Mais, (13) _____ été, il reste (14) _____ France, (15) _____ Bretagne!

Language points

Did you notice?

When Chantal told Anne what she and her husband were going to do, she used **on**:

***On* va visiter les monuments romains.**
We are going to visit the Roman monuments.

Though **on** can have other uses which you will no doubt discover later, it is often used in French to replace **nous** in informal speech.

You will hear the French use it a lot. When you use it, remember that it works like **il/elle**:

Il fait **du tennis.**
Elle fait **du tennis.**   *On fait* **du tennis.**

Il va **cinéma?**
Elle va **au cinéma?**   *On va* **au cinéma?**

Exercise 4

Answer the following questions, using **on**.

1 Vous allez à Paris?
   Oui, _____ .

2 Vous travaillez en France?
   Non, _____ .

3 Vous allez faire du yoga?
   Oui, _____ .

4 Vous avez l'intention de visiter la Thaïlande?
   Non, _____ .

Language points

Using connaître *and* savoir

Most of the time, both verbs are translated by *to know* in English. The difference between **savoir** and **connaître** is not always easy to grasp, even for French people! We will limit ourselves to some clear-cut uses, here.

You can use **connaître** when you talk about a person, place, subject or domain of which you have knowledge, or with which you are acquainted or familiar:

Vous *connaissez* **la Grèce?**
Elle *connaît* **Anne Murdoch.**
Je *connais* **bien la littérature française.**

Very often **connaître** is followed by a noun.

You can use **savoir** to talk about something you have practical knowlededge of or simply whenever you want to translate *you know*, or *I know* on their own:

Je *sais* nager.   – Il habite à Londres.
I can swim.   – Je *sais*.

Very often **savoir** is not followed by a noun.

Dialogue 2 🎧 (Audio 1; 37)

Location de voitures

Car rental

Anne visits the car rental agency to rent a car for the weekend.

ANNE: Bonjour, monsieur. Je voudrais louer une voiture, s'il vous plaît.
EMPLOYE: Oui, madame. Pour combien de jours?
ANNE: Pour le week-end. J'aimerais partir vendredi et rentrer dimanche ou lundi. Ah, oui, et je préfère une petite voiture, plutôt.
EMPLOYE: Alors, nous avons des offres spéciales en ce moment, des forfaits week-end de trois jours à 35 euros par jour.
ANNE: Tout compris?
EMPLOYE: Oui, madame, assurance et TVA comprises.
ANNE: Parfait.
EMPLOYE: Vous souhaitez réserver, madame?
ANNE: Oui, s'il vous plaît.
EMPLOYE: Vous avez une pièce d'identité et votre permis de conduire?
ANNE: Oui, voilà.
EMPLOYE: Merci. Alors, vous êtes madame Anne Murdoch ... et donc je vous réserve une voiture en catégorie A, du vendredi 10 au dimanche 12 août inclus. C'est bien ça?
ANNE: Oui, c'est ça.
EMPLOYE: Voilà, c'est réservé.

ANNE: *Hello, I would like to rent a car, please.*
ASSISTANT: *Yes, for how many days?*
ANNE: *For the weekend. I would like to leave on Friday and return on Sunday or Monday. Oh yes, and I prefer a small car.*

ASSISTANT:	*We have special offers at the moment, weekend pack-ages of three days, at 35 euros per day.*
ANNE:	*Everything included?*
ASSISTANT:	*Yes madam, insurance and VAT included.*
ANNE:	*That's perfect.*
ASSISTANT:	*Do you wish to book?*
ANNE:	*Yes, please.*
ASSISTANT:	*Do you have some ID and your driving licence?*
ANNE:	*Yes, here you are.*
ASSISTANT:	*Thank you. So, you are Mrs Anne Murdoch ... and I am booking a 'category A' car for you, from Friday 10 to Sunday 12 August included. Is that it?*
ANNE:	*Yes that's correct.*
ASSISTANT:	*That's booked for you.*

Language points

Asking for something and saying what you would like to do

You have already come across **je voudrais**.

Je voudrais un café, s'il vous plaît.
Je voudrais une soupe de poisson.

You can use **je voudrais** + another verb in the infinitive:

Je voudrais louer **une voiture**.
I would like to rent a car.

Je voudrais travailler **à Nice**.
I would like to work in Nice.

Je voudrais prendre **un taxi**.
I would like to take a taxi.

You can use **j'aimerais** in the same way.

J'aimerais un Coca®.
J'aimerais un steak-frites.   I would like steak and chips.

J'aimerais travailler à Paris.
J'aimerais prendre des vacances en mai.
J'aimerais rester à la maison.   I would like to stay at home.

Exercise 5

Combine one element from each column to make sentences.

Example: **Je voudrais prendre des vacances en octobre.**

je voudrais	prendre	à Londres
j'aimerais	louer	les arènes d'Arles
	travailler	un camping-car
	visiter	au cinéma
	aller	du karaté
	faire	des vacances en octobre

Language points

Talking about your movements

To talk about your movements, you can use **partir** and **rentrer**.

Je *pars* vendredi et je *rentre* dimanche.
I leave/am leaving on Friday and I am coming back
on Sunday.

Elle *part* en vacances mardi prochain.
She goes/is going on holiday next Tuesday.

Giving dates

As with months of the year, the days of the week do not have a capital letter in French. Dates are expressed using cardinal numbers (two, twenty-five, and so on) and not, as in English, ordinal numbers (second, twenty-fifth, and so on), the only exception being the first of the month: **le premier**. When giving a precise date, the French normally use the article **le** in front of it.

le 10 juin
le 24 janvier
le 5 février

le mardi 4 octobre
le dimanche 16 septembre
le samedi 12 mars

Les jours de la semaine
(days of the week)

 (Audio 1; 38)

lundi	Monday
mardi	Tuesday
mercredi	Wednesday
jeudi	Thursday
vendredi	Friday
samedi	Saturday
dimanche	Sunday

Je pars *le vendredi 10 juin.*
Je rentre *le mardi 14 juillet.*

Exercice 6 (Audio 1; 39)

Imagine you are making several trips to France this year. Using the model below, make sentences to say when you are going and coming back.

Example: **Je pars le 25 avril et je rentre le 2 mai.**

1	28/6	12/7
2	30/10	5/11
3	Friday 25 December	Wednesday 30
4	Monday 3 February	Thursday 6

Language points

More about dates

You can talk about the length of a project or a stay in this way:

Je pars en France *pour* trois jours.
I'm going to France for three days.

Je voudrais louer une voiture *pour* une semaine.
I would like to rent a car for a week.

You can also be more specific about the dates:

Je pars en France *du* **10 juillet** *au* **15 août.**
Je voudrais louer une voiture *du* **10** *au* **15 juillet.**

Exercise 7  (Audio 1; 40)

Read the information below about car rental.

1 How much would you pay for a three-day rental?
2 How much would you pay for a week?
3 Is everything included in the prices quoted?
4 What are the two conditions of this offer?
5 You want to rent a car for seven days. Your dates are 21 to 28 August. Prepare in writing what you would say in the car rental agency, then memorise it and say it aloud.

LOCATION DE VOITURES A PRIX DISCOUNT

Forfait week–end   **Forfait semaine**

35 euros TTC par jour   45 euros TTC par jour

pour 3 jours de location   pour 7 jours de location

Offres valables du 10 juillet au 20 août 2005 inclus

Réservation uniquement sur Internet

Cultural point

Some important dates in France

En France on ne travaille pas:

le 1er janvier   **le jour de l'an**   New Year's Day
le lundi de Pâques   Easter Monday

| **le 1ᵉʳ Mai** | **la fête du travail** | May Day |
| **le 8 Mai** | **la Victoire** | end of the Second World War |

le jeudi de l'Ascension et le lundi de Pentecôte

Both are religious celebrations the dates of which are linked with Easter Monday. They occur in May and June.

le 14 Juillet   **fête nationale**

It celebrates the fall of La Bastille in 1789 during the French Revolution.

le 15 août	**l'Assomption**	Assumption
le 1ᵉʳ novembre	**la Toussaint**	All Saints' Day
le 11 Novembre	**l'Armistice**	Armistice Day First World War
le 25 décembre	**Noël**	Christmas Day

The French are quite famous for their bank holidays (**jours fériés**) especially during the month of May, when up to four bank holidays can occur. When **un jour férié** is on a Thursday or Tuesday, the French will often **faire le pont**, literally take the Friday or Monday off to make a bridge between the two days they officially are not at work. Frequently, businesses will close to allow their employees to **faire le pont**. If a bank holiday falls on a weekend, there is no compensation.

6 Faire ses courses

Shopping

Dialogue 1 🎧 (Audio 1; 41)

Au supermarché

At the supermarket

Jacques and Chantal have arrived in their studio in Provence and go to a supermarket to do some basic shopping. Can you spot the two expressions they use to say what they need?

JACQUES: Tu as une liste?

CHANTAL: Oui, bien sûr! Alors, il nous faut du pain, du lait, du beurre, des yaourts, de l'eau minérale, du café, de la mayonnaise, de la moutarde, du papier toilettes ...

JACQUES: On a aussi besoin de gel douche et de dentifrice.

CHANTAL: Oui, tiens, est-ce que tu voudrais bien chercher le rayon petit déjeuner? Il faut aussi de la confiture et du pain de mie.

JACQUES: Je vais aussi regarder le vin pour ce soir.
CHANTAL: Bon, on se retrouve à la caisse, alors.
JACQUES: Oui, très bien.

[Chantal arrête une employée]

CHANTAL: Excusez-moi, madame, où se trouve la moutarde, s'il vous plaît?
EMPLOYEE: Avec l'huile et le vinaigre, madame. C'est un peu plus loin sur votre droite.
CHANTAL: Merci.

JACQUES: *Do you have a list?*
CHANTAL: *Yes, of course! So, we need bread, milk, butter, yoghurt, mineral water, coffee, mayonnaise, mustard, toilet paper . . .*
JACQUES: *We also need shower gel and toothpaste.*
CHANTAL: *Yes, look, would you like to look for the breakfast section? We also need jam and a sandwich loaf.*
JACQUES: *I am also going to have a look at wine for tonight.*
CHANTAL: *OK, so we'll meet at the checkout, then.*
JACQUES: *Fine.*

[Chantal stops an employee]

CHANTAL: *Excuse-me, where can I find mustard, please?*
EMPLOYEE: *With the oil and vinegar. They're a little further on on your right.*
CHANTAL: *Thank you.*

Language points

Did you notice?

Il (nous) faut *du* pain, *de l'*eau minérale et *de la* mayonnaise.
We need bread, mineral water and mayonnaise.

J'ai *de la* bière dans le frigo.
I have (some) beer in the fridge.

Du, **de la**, **de l'** are called partitive articles. You have already seen them in Unit 4 with the verb **faire: faire du vélo**. In the dialogue above they are used to list the things that Chantal and Jacques need to buy for the studio.

Masculine noun	Feminine noun	Noun starting with a vowel or an 'h'
du	de la	de l'

Exercise 1

Here is the list of items that Chantal and Jacques have already put in their trolley. Using the partitive articles, complete the sentence.

Ils ont du lait, _____

lait	café	dentifrice
pain	mayonnaise	huile
beurre	moutarde	vinaigre
eau minérale		

Language points

Saying what you need

To say what you need in French you can use two forms.

Il faut from the verb **falloir** can only be conjugated with **il**. **Il** does not stand for someone or something; it is only there to act as a subject of the verb. Only the context or the use of **me**, **te**, **nous**, and so on, placed between **il** and **faut**, will enable you to know who is being talked about.

You can use **il** (**me/te/nous** and so on) **faut** with a *noun* or another *verb* in the *infinitive*.

Il faut **du pain.**
One/you/we need(s) bread.

Il faut **travailler beaucoup.**
One/you/we need(s) to work a lot.

Il me faut **du thé.**
I need some tea.

Il nous faut **de la confiture.**
We need jam.

Il te faut **prendre des vacances.**
You need to take holidays.

Alternatively, you can use **avoir besoin de**:

J'ai besoin de **lait.**
I need milk.

Nous avons besoin **de miel et de biscuits.**
We need honey and biscuits.

Exercise 2 🎧 (Audio 1; 42)

Here is the rest of Jacques and Chantal's shopping list. Speaking as if you were Jacques or Chantal, make one sentence, using **il nous faut** and one sentence with **avoir besoin de** to say what you need to buy.

huile	Coca®
vinaigre	jus d'orange
sel (salt) (m.)	lessive (washing powder) (f.)
poivre (pepper) (m.)	viande (meat) (f.)

Language points

Shopping in French supermarkets

Où se trouve la moutarde, s'il vous plaît?
Where is/where can I find the mustard, please?

Excusez-moi, *je cherche* **le rayon céréales.**
Excuse me, I'm looking for the cereals section?

Here are some more sections you will be likely to find in a French supermarket.

l'électro-ménager	household electrical products
le bricolage	DIY
la papeterie	stationery
la librairie	book section
vêtements (hommes, femmes, enfants)	clothes (men, women, children)
chaussures	shoes
jardinage	gardening
aliments chiens et chats	dog/cat food
vaisselle	crockery

In the food sections, look out for:

le rayon des surgelés	frozen-food section
le rayon des conserves	tinned *or* preserved-food section

These items will also be useful:

la caisse	checkout
en réclame	on special offer
en promotion	on special offer
en solde	sale price

Cultural point

Hypermarchés and **supermarchés** are normally found on the out-skirts of towns and cities in France. They are usually well provided with fresh produce and offer excellent value for money. Though you will usually find most of the things you can find in Britain, some sections (**rayons**) will offer a much wider choice of products. This is especially the case for **le rayon des conserves** and, if you are in a French supermarket, do not forget to visit the section on **produits régionaux**. In order to prevent theft and avoid trolleys being abandoned after use, you will need a one euro coin to collect a trolley (**un caddy**) from a designated area. You will be able to get your coin back only if you take your trolley to a designated area. As most French supermarkets will have a petrol station, it is worth checking the price of petrol since it often tends to be lower than at the roadside stations.

Exercise 3 (Audio 1; 43)

You are in a French supermarket and are looking for the following things. Stop an employee and ask where they are.

1 mineral water
2 stationery
3 frozen-food section
4 mayonnaise
5 salt
6 tinned-food section

Dialogue 2 🎧 (Audio 1; 44)

Au marché

At the market

Jacques and Chantal, like a lot of French people, prefer to buy fresh produce in the market. They are now at a fruit and vegetable stall. Pay attention to the expressions of quantity.

MARCHAND:	C'est à vous madame?
CHANTAL:	Oui. Je voudrais un kilo de tomates, s'il vous plaît ... une botte de carottes aussi. Ah oui, et on prend aussi des pêches blanches. C'est combien le kilo?
MARCHAND:	4 euros, madame.
CHANTAL:	Parfait. Un kilo, alors.
JACQUES:	Tu n'achètes pas de cerises? Tu adores ça!
CHANTAL:	Si, mais juste un petit peu, elles sont chères.
MARCHAND:	500 grammes, madame?
CHANTAL:	Oui, très bien et un peu de persil aussi, s'il vous plaît.
MARCHAND:	Ce sera tout?

CHANTAL: Donnez-moi aussi une salade, s'il vous plaît ... la romaine là-bas.
MARCHAND: Voilà, madame.
CHANTAL: Combien je vous dois?
MARCHAND: Ça vous fait 15 euros 65.

MARCHAND: *Are you next, madam?*
CHANTAL: *Yes, I would like a kilo of tomatoes, please ... a bunch of carrots too. Oh yes, we will also have some white peaches. How much is a kilo?*
MARCHAND: *4 euros.*
CHANTAL: *Fine. One kilo, then.*
JACQUES: *You're not buying any cherries? You love them!*
CHANTAL: *Yes, but just a few, they're expensive.*
MARCHAND: *500 grammes?*
CHANTAL: *Yes, fine and a little parsley too, please.*
MARCHAND: *Is that everything?*
CHANTAL: *Give me a lettuce, too, please ... the cos over there.*
MARCHAND: *There you are.*
CHANTAL: *How much do I owe you?*
MARCHAND: *It's 15 euros 65.*

Language points

Talking about quantities

You can use precise measures:

un kilo de **pommes**	*500 grammes de* **cerises**
a kilo of apples	500 grammes of cherries
un litre de **lait**	*un demi-litre de* **vin**
a litre of milk	half a litre of wine

The French use the metric system: 1 kilogram is roughly the equivalent of 2.2 lbs and a litre is just under two pints. When shopping, the French will often use **une livre** to express 500 grammes.

une livre de **haricots verts**
500 grammes/half a kilo of green beans

You will also find these useful:

une tranche de **pain**	a slice of bread
un morceau de **fromage**	a piece of cheese

une bouteille de **vin**	a bottle of wine
une boîte de **cœurs** **d'artichauts**	a tin of artichoke hearts
un paquet de **biscuits**	a packet of biscuits
une plaque de **beurre/** **chocolat**	a packet of butter/a bar of chocolate

You can also use:

| *un peu de* **vin** | *beaucoup de* **tomates** |
| a little wine | a lot of tomatoes |

Remember that *all expressions of quantities are followed by* **de**.

Exercise 4

Pick out the nonsense quantities in the following:

J'aimerais ...   1 une livre de pommes.
2 10 grammes d'oranges.
3 deux litres de parfum.
4 une bouteille de persil.
5 un paquet de chips (crisps).
6 un morceau de gâteau.
7 une tranche de bière.
8 une plaque de viande.

Exercise 5 (Audio 1; 45)

Look at the shopping list below. You go first to the fruit and vegetable stall and then to the fishmonger to buy what you need. Using the expressions provided and the list, talk to the stallholders, asking them for various items.

tomates (1 kg)
abricots (1 livre)
cerises (200 g)
avocats (2)
persil (un peu)
thon (4 tranches)
crevettes (300 g)
truites (2)

je voudrais ...
j'aimerais ...
donnez-moi ...

Language points

Using ne . . . pas de

You will need to remember that **ne . . . pas de** is also an expression of quantity:

> **Tu *n*'achètes *pas de* cerises?**

> **Vous avez des pommes?**
> **Non, je *n*'ai *pas de* pommes.**

> **Dans mon frigo, j'ai de la bière et du Coca® mais je *n*'ai *pas d*'eau minérale.**
> In my fridge, I have beer and Coke but I don't have any mineral water.

So, when talking about quantities, all the articles **un**, **une**, **des** and **du**, **de la**, **de l'** will normally change to **de** when you use **ne . . . pas**.

Exercise 6 (Audio 1; 46)

Say that you have, and then that you do not have the following items in your house.

> *Example*: **J'ai de la bière.**
> **Je n'ai pas de bière.**

1 vin
2 moutarde
3 eau minérale
4 café
5 chips
6 yaourts
7 lait
8 thon

Language points

Paying for what you buy (Audio 1; 47)

The French adopted the euro in January 2002. All prices are now displayed in euros, but you might still hear people speaking in francs or converting back to francs whenever they are not sure of the value of something. On price labels, decimals will appear after a coma, for example: **43,50 euros**.

un billet de 5 euros	a 5 euro note
un billet de 20 euros	a 20 euro note
une pièce de 2 euros	a 2 euro coin
une pièce de 50 centimes	a 50 cent coin

To ask for the price of something, you can say:

Ça fait combien?	**Je vous dois combien?**
How much is it?	How much do I owe you?
C'est combien?	**Ça coûte combien?**
How much is it?	How much does it cost?

You will hear people answer you in these ways:

45 euros, **monsieur.**	*Ça fait* **67 euros 50.**
	It's 67 euros 50.
Ça coûte **23 euros.**	**C'est 5 euros.**
It costs 23 euros.	It's 5 euros.

Other useful expressions include:

Vous avez la monnaie?
Do you have the right change?

Non *je n'ai pas la monnaie.*
No, I do not have the right change.

Vous avez de la monnaie?
Do you have any small change?

Non, *je n'ai pas de monnaie.*
No, I don't have any change.

Vous payez en liquide?	Are you paying cash?
par carte de crédit?	by credit card
par chèque?	by cheque

Vous prenez les cartes de crédit?
Do you take credit cards?

Exercise 7

C'est combien? Say the following prices out loud.

17,50 euros	4,80 euros
58 euros	150,90 euros

Exercise 8

Pair the question with its answer.

1 Combien je vous dois?

   (a) J'ai un billet de 50 euros. C'est tout.

2 Vous avez des pommes vertes?

   (b) Non, un kilo, s'il vous plaît.

3 Vous avez la monnaie?

   (c) Non, je n'ai pas de pommes, aujourd'hui.

4 Une livre de tomates, c'est bien ça?

   (d) Ça vous fait 32,67 euros.

5 Vous prenez les cartes de crédit?

   (e) Non, juste du liquide, madame.

7 Planifier un voyage d'affaires

Planning a business trip

> **In this unit you will learn about:**
>
> - **savoir**, **pouvoir**, **vouloir** and **devoir**
> - telling the time with the 24-hour clock
> - comparing things
> - using adjectives
> - asking questions with **est-ce que**

Dialogue 1 🎧 (Audio 1; 48)

Grenoble-Paris

A few months later, Anne is in Grenoble and plans to go to Paris on a business trip. She rings a local travel agency to organise her trip.

ANNE: Oui, allô, bonjour. Je dois aller quelques jours à Paris, pour un voyage d'affaires.

EMPLOYE: Oui, madame. Vous voulez prendre le train ou vous préférez l'avion?

ANNE: Ben, euh... je ne sais pas. Ça dépend du prix, je suppose.

EMPLOYE: Vous connaissez la date de votre départ et de votre retour?

ANNE: Oui. Alors, je dois absolument partir le vendredi 31 octobre pour être à Paris vers 14 heures au plus tard.

J'ai une réunion à 15 heures 30... Pour le retour, je suis plus flexible. Je peux rentrer le mardi 4 ou le mercredi 5 novembre.

EMPLOYE: Alors, vous avez un vol direct pour Paris à 10 heures 50. Arrivée à Paris Orly 12 heures 10. Le vol retour au départ d'Orly est à 16 heures 40, arrivée à Grenoble 18 heures. Le billet aller-retour fait 260 euros.

ANNE: Eh bien! C'est vraiment pas donné! Et le train?

EMPLOYE: Vous pouvez prendre un TGV direct pour Paris à 10 heures 34, arrivée à Paris 13 heures 35 pour 77 euros 70. Attendez, il y a encore moins cher. Vous pouvez aussi prendre un train à 10 heures 10 et être à Paris à 13 heures 55 pour 63 euros 30. Mais vous devez changer à Lyon.

ANNE: C'est moins cher mais moins pratique. Pour le TGV, il faut impérativement réserver, non?

EMPLOYE: C'est bien ça, madame. Vous devez réserver votre place, mais la réservation est gratuite.

ANNE: *Hello. I have to go to Paris on a business trip for a few days.*

EMPLOYEE: *Yes, madam. Do you want to travel by train or do you prefer to fly?*

ANNE: *Well, er ... I don't know. I suppose it depends on the price.*

EMPLOYEE: *Do you know when you want to go and come back?*

ANNE: *Yes, I absolutely must leave on Friday, 31 October to be in Paris around 2 p.m. at the latest. I have a meeting at 3.30 p.m. ... I am more flexible for the return date. I can return on Tuesday, 4 November or Wednesday, 5.*

EMPLOYEE: *Well, you have a direct flight to Paris at 10.50, arriving at Paris Orly at 12.10. The return flight from Orly is at 16.40, arriving in Grenoble at 18.00. The price of the return ticket is 260 euros.*

ANNE: *Wow! That's not cheap! What about trains?*

EMPLOYEE: *You can take a direct TGV to Paris at 10.34, arriving in Paris at 13.35 for 77.70 euros. Wait, there's something even cheaper. You can take a train at 10.10 and be in Paris at 13.55 for 66.30 euros. But you have to change in Lyon.*

ANNE: *It's cheaper but less convenient. For the TGV, booking is compulsory, isn't it?*

EMPLOYEE: *Yes madam, you must reserve your seat, but booking is free of charge.*

Language points

Saying what you can do

To say what you can do or cannot do, you can use **pouvoir** in the present tense.

In all cases, **pouvoir** will be followed by another *verb* in the *infinitive*, unless that verb is implied.

> **Tu *peux* venir dimanche?**
> Can you come on Sunday?
>
> **Je *peux* (venir), oui.**
> I can (come), yes.

When you want to use the verb in the negative form, **ne ... pas** will be placed on either side of **pouvoir**.

> **Il *ne* peut *pas* partir vendredi.**
> He cannot leave on Friday

The verb pouvoir

Je **peux** louer une voiture.

Tu **peux** rentrer samedi?

Il/elle/on **peut** arriver ce soir.

Nous pouv**ons** réserver une table.

Vous pouv**ez** aller au cinéma.

Ils/elles peuv**ent** partir en train.

Be careful!

In English, we use **can** to mean *to know how to do something*. In these cases, the French will use **savoir**:

Vous *savez* nager?	**Il *sait* monter à cheval.**
Can you swim?	He can ride.
Elles *savent* bien cuisiner.	**Je ne *sais* pas conduire.**
They can cook well.	I can't drive.

Exercise 1

True or false? **Vrai ou faux?**

Un enfant de trois ans ...

1 sait conduire.
2 peut regarder des films violents.
3 sait marcher.
4 peut voter.
5 sait parler.
6 ne sait pas faire la cuisine.
7 ne peut pas sortir tout seul.

Now, fill in the gaps with a correct form of **pouvoir** and **savoir**.

8 Vous _____ arriver vers 8 heures?
9 Je ne _____ pas piloter un avion.
10 Elle _____ rentrer dimanche.
11 Tu _____ louer une voiture pour le week-end.
12 Nous _____ danser le tango argentin.
13 Ils _____ venir le mois prochain.

Language points

Did you notice?

In previous units, you came across **je voudrais** to request something in a polite way.

Je *voudrais* un café, s'il vous plaît.

Here, in the dialogue, the travel agent uses another form of the same verb, **vouloir**, to ask what Anne wants to do. It is a form of **vouloir** in the present tense.

Vous *voulez* prendre le train?
Do you want to travel by train?

Vouloir in the present tense follows the same pattern as **pouvoir**:

Je *veux* partir tôt.
I want to leave early.

Nous ne *voulons* pas manger ici.
We don't want to eat here.

Elles *veulent* un thé au citron.
They want a lemon tea.

Did you notice that **vouloir** can be followed by a **noun** or another **verb** in the **infinitive?**

Saying what you have to do

To say what you *have to do* or *must do*, you can use **devoir** or **il faut** (which you met in Unit 6) in the present tense. Like **pouvoir**, **devoir** is always followed by another *verb* in the *infinitive*.

Sur le TGV, *il faut* réserver.
On the TGV, one/you must/have to reserve a seat.

Je *dois* partir à 8 heures.
I must/have to leave at 8.

Nous *devons* prendre un train.
We must/have to take a train.

Il *ne* doit *pas* réserver une place.
He doesn't have to book a seat.

The verb devoir **(must)**

Je **dois** partir.

Tu **dois** rentrer.

Il/elle/on **doit** réserver.

Nous dev**ons** louer une voiture.

Vous dev**ez** rester à Paris.

Ils/elles doiv**ent** partir.

Exercise 2 🎧 (Audio 1; 50)

You have been invited to do a number of things. Follow the model and make excuses, using **devoir**.

> *Example*: **Vous voulez jouer au golf demain?**
> **Je ne peux pas. Je dois aller à Paris.**

1 Vous voulez manger avec moi?

Je ne peux pas. _____
(say you have to go shopping)

2 Vous voulez aller au cinéma, ce soir?

Je ne peux pas. _____
(say you have to go to the restaurant with Anne)

3 Vous voulez prendre l'apéritif?

_____
(say you can't: you have to leave)

Language points

Telling the time with the 24-hour clock

The 24-hour clock is used more and more in French, especially when giving times of trains, flights, buses or programmes.

Le premier train part à *15 h 10*.
The first train leaves at 15.30.

Il arrive à *20 h 56*.
It arrives at 20.56.

Le film commence à *20 h 35*.
The film starts at 20.35.

The letter **h** stands for **heure(s)** (hours), and when you say the following times out loud, you should pronounce it. Hence you should say for:

18 h 15   **dix-huit heures quinze**

9 h 45   **neuf heures quarante-cinq**

Exercise 3

Read out loud the times printed on this timetable.

numéro du TGV	5600	5765	6821
Grenoble	10:10	11:28	
Lyon-Part-Dieu	11:56	12:12	
Avignon (gare TGV)		13:21	
Marseille		13:58	14:55
Toulon			15:47
Cannes			17:08
Nice			17:39

Now fill in the gaps with the missing verbs and times.

1 Le train de Grenoble _____ à Lyon à 11 h 56.
2 Le TGV 5765 _____ de Grenoble à 11 h 28 et il _____ à
   Marseille à 13 h 58.
3 Le TGV 6821 _____ de Marseille à _____ et il _____ à Nice
   à _____ .

Language points

Comparing things

Regardless of the adjectives you use in French, you use **plus**
(meaning 'more'), **moins** (meaning 'less') and **aussi** (meaning 'as')
to make comparisons. So, it is actually a lot simpler in French than
in English.

Pour le retour, je suis *plus* flexible.
For the return, I am more flexible.

Attendez, il y a encore *moins* cher.
Wait, there's even cheaper.

C'est *moins* cher mais *moins* pratique.
It's cheaper but less convenient.

**Tu veux vraiment prendre l'avion? En fait, le train est
aussi rapide.**
Do you really want to fly? In fact, the train is *as* fast.

You can also use **que** (here meaning 'than' or 'as') when you want
to make it absolutely clear what you are comparing:

**Le train est *aussi* rapide *que* l'avion. Il est *moins* cher
(*que* l'avion).**
Travelling by train is *as* fast *as* flying. It's *cheaper*
(*than* going by plane).

Exercise 4

Read the dialogue again and then correct these false statements.

1 L'avion est moins cher que le train.
2 Le train de 10 h 34 est aussi rapide que le train de 10 h 10.
3 Le train de 10 h 34 est moins cher.
4 Pour Anne, le train de 10 h 10 est plus pratique mais il est plus
   cher.

Dialogue 2 ⌒ (Audio 1; 52)

Projets de week-end

Weekend plans

*Anne also intends to mix business with pleasure. Her trip to Paris
will give her the opportunity to spend a few days with a French
friend of hers, Malika. Anne rings Malika to tell her she is coming.
We pick up the conversation as they are talking about their plans
for the weekend.*

MALIKA: A quelle heure est-ce que tu es libre vendredi soir?
ANNE: Normalement, je dois être libre vers 18 heures 30.
MALIKA: Je connais un bon petit restaurant grec . . . ils font une
          moussaka délicieuse! Ça te dit?
ANNE: Quelle bonne idée! Où est-ce qu'il est, ce restaurant?
MALIKA: Dans le Quartier Latin.

ANNE: Parfait, c'est vraiment pas loin. Samedi, j'ai envie de
           faire un peu de shopping! J'ai besoin d'une nouvelle
           robe et de chaussures confortables.

MALIKA: Alors, là, pas de problèmes. On peut aller faire les
           magasins sur les boulevards ou, si tu veux, on peut
           aussi aller dans le Quartier des Halles. Il y a des
           petites boutiques sympathiques. J'ai aussi deux billets
           pour une exposition intéressante. C'est une exposition
           de vieilles photographies de Paris. Elle commence
           mercredi. Quand est-ce que tu rentres à Grenoble?

ANNE: Mardi, malheureusement.

MALIKA: *What time are you free on Friday evening?*

ANNE: *I normally ought to be free around half past six.*

MALIKA: *I know a good little Greek restaurant ... they make a
           delicious moussaka. How about that?*

ANNE: *What a good idea! Where is this restaurant?*

MALIKA: *In the Latin Quarter.*

ANNE: *Perfect, it's really not far. On Saturday, I feel like doing
           some shopping! I need a new dress and comfortable
           shoes.*

MALIKA: *No problem. We can go shopping on the boulevards,
           or if you want, we can also go to the Halles. There are
           some nice little shops there. I also have two tickets
           for an interesting exhibition. It's an exhibition of old
           pictures of Paris. It starts on Wednesday. When are you
           going back to Grenoble?*

ANNE: *On Tuesday, unfortunately.*

Language points

Describing people and things

You can describe people or things with adjectives. In French, the
adjective will agree in gender (masculine or feminine) and number
(singular or plural) with the noun it is used with. Usually this means
that, unless it already ends with an **-e** in its masculine form, the
adjective will end with an **-e** if it is used with a feminine noun.
And normally, unless it already ends with an **-s** or an **-x** in its

singular form, it will end with an **-s** when it is used with a noun in the plural.

C'est *un livre intéressant.*
It's an interesting book.

C'est *une exposition intéressante.*
It's an interesting exhibition.

Elle achète *des livres intéressants.*
She buys interesting books.

Elle va à *des expositions intéressantes.*
She goes to interesting exhibitions.

There are other patterns. Here are a few to start you with:

Masculine	→	Feminine
bo*n*, italie*n* ...	ne	bon*ne*, italien*ne*
nature*l*, actue*l* (current)	le	naturel*le*, actuel*le*
neu*f* (new), attenti*f* ...	ve	neu*ve*, attenti*ve*
délici*eux*, séri*eux* ...	euse	délici*euse*, séri*euse*
premi*er*, étrang*er* (foreign) ...	ère	premi*ère*, étrang*ère*

All adjectives whose masculine form ends in **-eau**, will take an **-x** in the masculine plural.

Il y a un nouv*eau* film au cinéma.
There's a new film at the cinema.

Elle aime bien ses nouveau*x* amis.
She likes her new friends.

There are also a few exceptions:

Singular		Plural		
Masculine	Feminine	Masculine	Feminine	
beau	belle	beaux	belles	(beautiful)
vieux/vieil	vieille	vieux	vieilles	(old)
long	longue	longs	longues	(long)
faux	fausse	faux	fausses	(wrong/insincere)
frais	fraîche	frais	fraîches	(fresh)

The position of adjectives

The normal position for adjectives in French is after the noun.

Il y a un film *français* à la télévision, ce soir.

Il achète toujours des voitures *étrangères*.

However, the adjectives **beau**, **bon**, **grand**, **petit**, **jeune** (young), **joli**, **vieux**, **long**, **dernier** (last), **gros** (big), **nouveau** are generally placed before the noun.

C'est une *bonne* idée!
It's a good idea.

C'est un *bon petit* restaurant.

Exercise 5

In the sentences below, choose the form of the adjectives given in brackets which fits the gap.

1 Ils ont une voiture _____ .
   (nouveau, anglaise, grande)
2 C'est un _____ film.
   (bon, nouvelle, français)
3 J'ai un _____ problème.
   (dernière, facile, petit)
4 Je préfère les vins _____ .
   (rouge, australiens, américaines)
5 Le TGV est un train _____ .
   (nouveau, rapide, bon)

Language points

Asking questions with est-ce que

In the first unit, you learned one way of asking questions in French. You can also use **est-ce que** to ask a question in French. Both of these ways are used in standard French.

Tu aimes le poisson?
or *Est-ce que* **tu aimes le poisson?**
Do you like fish?

Vous êtes anglaise?
or *Est-ce que* **vous êtes anglaise?**
Are you English?

With **quand** (when), **à quelle heure** (what time), **où** (where), **combien** (how much), **qui** (who) and **quoi** or **que** (what), this is how it works:

Question word	Rising intonation	Est-ce que
quand	**Tu rentres** *quand*?	*Quand* **est-ce que tu rentres?**
à quelle heure	**Tu es libre** *à quelle heure*?	*A quelle heure* **est-ce que tu es libre?**
où	**Il arrive** *où*?	*Où* **est-ce qu'il arrive?**
combien	**Ça coûte** *combien*?	*Combien* **est-ce que ça coûte?**
qui	**Tu invites** *qui*?	*Qui* **est-ce que tu invites?**
quoi/que	**Tu fais** *quoi*?	*Qu'*est-ce que **tu fais?**

Exercise 6 🎧 (Audio 1; 54)

Using both ways of asking questions, provide the questions to the answers below.

Example: **Je rentre à Paris** *vendredi*.
Tu rentres/vous rentrez à Paris *quand*?
Quand est-ce que **tu rentres/vous rentrez à Paris?**

1 Elle part *dimanche*.
2 Je vais *en France* au mois de juillet.
3 Ça coûte *35 euros*.
4 Ils invitent *Pierre et Marie*.
5 Le train part *à 20 h 25*.
6 Marie veut acheter *des chaussures confortables*.

Exercise 7

You want to travel from Grenoble to Nice. Prepare five questions with **est-ce que** to enquire about time of departure and arrival, and where you must change.

Le vieux Nice

8 Quel voyage!

What a journey!

> **In this unit you will learn about:**
>
> * the **passé composé** with **avoir** (perfect tense)
> * telling the time with the 12-hour clock
> * talking about your family
> * using possessive adjectives
> * using demonstrative adjectives

Dialogue 1 (Audio 1; 55)

J'ai oublié ma valise dans le taxi

I left my suitcase in the taxi

Anne has now arrived in Paris and meets Malika. Her trip has been a little more eventful than planned. Can you understand what happened to her?

MALIKA: Alors, ton voyage s'est bien passé?

ANNE: Ne m'en parle pas! Je suis arrivée à Paris avec une heure de retard. A la gare, j'ai pris un taxi pour aller plus vite. Et devine quoi? J'ai oublié ma valise dans le taxi.

MALIKA: Comment tu as fait, alors?

ANNE: J'ai appelé la compagnie de taxis et heureusement, ils ont trouvé le chauffeur tout de suite.

MALIKA: Et ta réunion?

ANNE: Ben, elle n'a pas commencé avant quatre heures et demie. C'est pour ça que je suis un peu en retard. Excuse-moi.

MALIKA: C'est pas grave. Mais, moi, je meurs de faim. Pas toi?

MALIKA: *So, did you have a good journey?*
ANNE: *Oh my goodness! I arrived in Paris an hour late. At the*
          station, I took a taxi to save time. And guess what? I left
          my suitcase in the taxi.
MALIKA: *So what did you do?*
ANNE: *I phoned the taxi company and luckily, they found the*
          driver straight away.
MALIKA: *And your meeting?*
ANNE: *Well, it didn't start until half past four. That's why I'm*
          a little late. Sorry.
MALIKA: *That's all right. But I'm starving. Aren't you?*

Language points

Talking about the past with the passé composé *(perfect tense)*

How to form the passé composé

In most cases, the **passé composé** (perfect tense) is formed by combining the present tense of **avoir** and a form of the main verb known as its **past participle**:

J'*ai pris* un taxi.

J'*ai oublié* ma valise.

Nous *avons mangé* au restaurant.

Although, in this unit, we will concentrate only on verbs following this pattern, reflexive verbs and a small number of other verbs use **être** instead of **avoir** when used in the **passé composé**. A full list of these will be given in the next unit. Did you spot the two examples used by Anne and Malika?

Ton voyage *s'est bien passé*?

Je *suis arrivée* à Paris avec une heure de retard.

So, to form the passé composé, you will need to know:

• whether to use **avoir** or **être**;
• the **past participle** form of the verb you want to use.

All **-er** verbs have their past participle end in **-é**:

manger	**mang***é*
aller	**all***é*
aimer	**aim***é*

Most **-ir** verbs have their past participle end in **-i**.

finir	**fin***i*
partir	**part***i*
servir	**serv***i*

Though **-u** is also a frequent ending, as always with French there are quite a few exceptions! Here is a list of most useful verbs you will need to memorise:

venir	to come	**venu**
vendre	to sell	**vendu**
prendre	to take	**pris**
faire	to do/make	**fait**
avoir	to have	**eu**
être	to be	**été**
pouvoir	to be able to	**pu**
devoir	to have to	**dû**
vouloir	to want	**voulu**
dire	to say	**dit**
entendre	to hear	**entendu**
voir	to see	**vu**
mettre	to put	**mis**

When to use the passé composé

Though the **passé composé** can generally be translated into English by the two forms below, depending on the context, those two forms in English will not necessarily be translated by the **passé composé**. So, relying on the English to choose when to use the **passé composé** might prove a little treacherous:

> **J'ai téléphoné à Marie.**
> I *rang* Marie.
> *or*   I *have rung* Marie.

Try to use the **passé composé** only when you recount *key events* that happened in the past. When you talk about past events or states, what you say generally includes key events and secondary information, usually of a descriptive nature, which are there to flesh out a story. In the story below, all key events have been underlined. In French, only the verbs in italics would be in the **passé composé**.

> I _rang_ Marie yesterday. She was very tired and was watching a film on TV. I _invited_ her out to see a band in a pub. A very well-known guitar player was performing. You know, when she was young, she played the guitar really well! After some persuasion, I finally _managed_ to convince her to come out with me.

Did you notice that 'played' would not be translated by a **passé composé**?

Exercise 1

Fill in the gaps putting the verbs in brackets in the **passé composé**.

1 J' _____ (manger) au restaurant.

2 Il _____ (faire) des courses.

3 Nous _____ (jouer) au tennis.

4 Vous _____ (prendre) le train?

5 Ils _____ (acheter) un sofa.

6 Tu _____ (visiter) le musée Grévin?

7 On _____ (avoir) un problème.

Exercise 2 (Audio 1; 56)

Read Dialogue 1 again and try to memorise Anne's adventures. Can you retell them, using the prompts below?

Elle est arrivée avec une heure de retard. Elle ...

> prendre un taxi
>
> oublier sa valise dans le taxi
>
> appeler la compagnie de taxis
>
> trouver le chauffeur

Language points

Did you notice?

When you want to use **ne ... pas** with a verb in the **passé composé**, **ne ... pas** is placed on each side of **avoir** or **être**.

> **Et ta réunion?**
> **Elle *n*'a *pas* commencé avant quatre heures et demie.**

> **Nous *ne* sommes *pas* arrivés à l'heure.**
> We didn't arrive/haven't arrived on time.

Exercise 3

Put the sentences from Exercise 1 into the negative form.

Exercise 4

Here's a list of things Max had to do for his manager. He has ticked what he did and put a cross against the things he could not do. Using the **passé composé**, write sentences to explain what he has done and what he has not done.

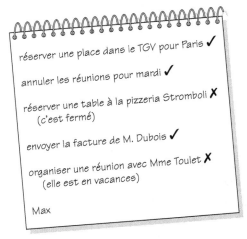

réserver une place dans le TGV pour Paris ✓

annuler les réunions pour mardi ✓

réserver une table à la pizzeria Stromboli ✗
   (c'est fermé)

envoyer la facture de M. Dubois ✓

organiser une réunion avec Mme Toulet ✗
   (elle est en vacances)

Max

annuler	to cancel	**envoyer**	to send
une facture	an invoice	**fermé**	closed

Language points

Telling the time with the 12-hour clock

The 12-hour clock is used in social situations. To ask for the time
you can say:

Excusez-moi, madame, vous avez l'heure, s'il vous plaît?
Excuse me, can you tell me the time, please?

Quelle heure est-il?
or **Il est quelle heure?**

What time is it?

Il est *une heure*.   It's *one o'clock*.
Il est *deux heures*.   It's *two o'clock*.

And so on.

Il est *midi*.   It's *twelve noon*.
Il est *minuit*.   It's *midnight*.

Il est onze heures *et quart*.
It's *quarter past* eleven.

Il est huit heures *moins le quart*.
It's *quarter to* eight.
Il est six heures *et demie*.
It's *half past* six.

Il est dix heures *cinq*.
It's *five past* ten.

Il est deux heures *moins dix*.
It's *ten to* two.

And so on.

The French do not use a.m. and p.m. But they can specify what
the time of day is by using the following:

Il est deux heures *du matin*.
It's two in the morning.

Il est trois heures *de l'après-midi*.
It's three in the afternoon.

Il est huit heures *du soir*.
It's eight in the evening.

Exercise 5

How would you say the following times with the 12-hour clock?

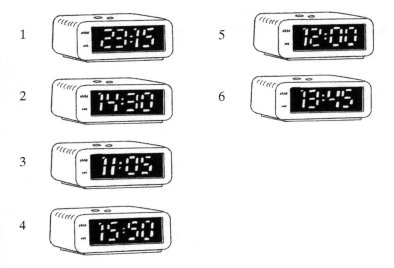

Dialogue 2 🎧 (Audio 1; 58)

Photos de famille

Family pictures

Malika shows Anne a few photos of her family. Listen to the dialogue and look at Malika's family tree.

MALIKA: Là, tu vois, c'est mon grand-père Ahmed. Il a 75 ans. Il est bien pour son âge, non?
ANNE: Oui, c'est impressionnant, dis donc! Et là, c'est ta grand-mère?
MALIKA: Oui. Et sur cette photo, c'est mon frère Nasser avec sa femme Sonia et mon neveu Benjamin. Il est mignon comme tout.

ANNE: Et ça, qui c'est?

MALIKA: Alors, là, c'est le mari de Clara, ma cousine, avec sa fille Sophie.

ANNE: Et tes parents, ils sont où?

MALIKA: Mes parents sont sur cette photo, avec ma sœur Julie.

ANNE: Ils ont l'air vraiment jeunes!

MALIKA: Ben, ils ont quand-même 52 ans! Mais, c'est vrai, ma mère fait très jeune surtout. Et tu vois, là, c'est Gina, la femme de Nedim, mon oncle. Elle est adorable. C'est une Italienne.

MALIKA: *Here, you see, that's my grandfather Ahmed. He's 75. He looks good for his age, doesn't he?*

ANNE: *Yes, it's amazing! And this is your grandmother?*

MALIKA: *Yes. And in this picture is my brother Nasser with his wife Sonia and my nephew Benjamin. He's really cute.*

ANNE: *And who's this?*

MALIKA: *That's Clara's husband – she's my cousin – with his daughter Sophie.*

ANNE: *And where are your parents?*

MALIKA: *My parents are in this picture with my sister Julie.*

ANNE: *They look really young.*

MALIKA: *Oh, they're both 52! But it's true, my mother especially looks very young. And you see, here is Gina, Nedim's wife – he's my uncle. She's adorable. She's Italian.*

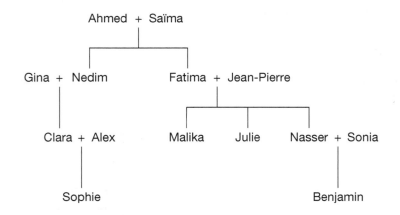

Language points

Family members

Masculine		Feminine	
le grand-père	grandfather	**la grand-mère**	grandmother
le père	father	**la mère**	mother
le fils	son	**la fille**	daughter
le mari	husband	**la femme**	wife
le frère	brother	**la sœur**	sister
le cousin	cousin	**la cousine**	cousin
l'oncle	uncle	**la tante**	aunt
le neveu	nephew	**la nièce**	niece
le beau-frère	brother-in-law	**la belle-sœur**	sister-in-law
le beau-père	father-in-law	**la belle-mère**	mother-in-law
le beau-fils	son-in-law	**la belle-fille**	daughter-in-law

Expressing connections with de

You can do it using **de** to link the nouns:

Nasser est le mari *de* Sonia.
Nasser is Sonia's husband.

Malika est la fille *de* Fatima et Jean-Pierre.
Malika is Fatima's and Jean-Pierre's daughter.

De will drop its **-e** in front of a noun starting with a vowel or an 'h'.

La mère *d'*Anne est écossaise.

You can also use this structure (always linking two nouns) in many other contexts.

- to express ownership:

  La voiture *de* Malika est rouge.
  Malika's car is red.

  La télévision *de* mes parents ne marche plus.
  My parents' television doesn't work any more.

- to give more detail about the nature of something:

> **Anne a appelé la compagnie *de* taxis.**
> Anne rang/has rung the taxi company.

> **J'ai acheté une housse *de* couette.**
> I bought/have bought a quilt cover.

> **Tu as mon numéro *de* téléphone?**
> Do you have my phone number?

Exercise 6 (Audio 1; 59)

Look at Malika's family tree and explain who these people are in relation to each other.

> *Example*: **Ahmed et Saïma**
>   **Ahmed est le mari de Saïma.**

1 Ahmed et Nedim   5 Clara et Malika
2 Clara et Gina   6 Nedim et Julie
3 Malika et Nedim   7 Jean-Pierre et Benjamin
4 Nasser et Malika

Language points

Expressing connections with possessive adjectives

You can also express connections and ownership with the possessive adjectives listed below. You will notice that their form changes, pretty much like the articles, according to the gender and number of the noun(s) they are used with. So for instance *my* can be translated by three different words: **mon, ma, mes**.

> **C'est *mon* frère.**
> It's *my* brother.

> ***Ma* mère s'appelle Magali.**
> *My* mother's name is Magali.

> **Pierre et Sandra sont *mes* amis.**
> Pierre and Sandra are *my* friends.

| Owner | Singular | | Plural |
	Masculine	Feminine	
je	*mon* **frère**	*ma* **sœur**	*mes* **parents**
tu	*ton* **oncle**	*ta* **tante**	*tes* **frères**
il/elle	*son* **mari**	*sa* **femme**	*ses* **sœurs**

Note also that **mon**, **ton** and **son** will be used in front of a feminine noun in the singular starting with a vowel or an **h**:

Anna?
C'est *mon* **ami***e***.**

Note that French does not differentiate between *his* and *her*. Both are translated by **son**, **sa** or **ses**.

It's his sister.
C'est *sa* **sœur.**

It's her sister.
C'est *sa* **sœur.**

The situation is a little simpler with **nous**, **vous**, **ils** and **elles** where there are only two forms, one for the singular, one for the plural.

Owner	Singular	Plural
nous	*notre* **fils** *notre* **fille**	*nos* **enfants**
vous	*votre* **mari** *votre* **grand-mère**	*vos* **nièces**
ils/elles	*leur* **frère** *leur* **sœur**	*leurs* **amis**

Exercise 7

Now, using the possessive adjectives, explain who these people are.

1 Vous êtes Ahmed. (a) Qui est Fatima?
 (b) Qui est Nedim?
 (c) Qui est Gina?

2 Vous êtes Julie.

(a) Qui est Nasser?
(b) Qui est Benjamin?
(c) Qui sont Fatima et Jean-Pierre?

3 Vous parlez de Nasser. (you are talking about Nasser)

(a) Qui est Jean-Pierre?
(b) Qui sont Julie et Malika?
(c) Qui est Saïma?

Language points

Did you notice?

Mes parents sont sur *cette* photo.
My parents are in this/that picture.

When you need to refer to someone or something that is present in a situation or that you have already talked about, you can use **ce**, **cette**, **ces**. They are called the demonstrative adjectives. As with the possessive adjectives, the demonstratives change their form according to the number and gender of the nouns they are used with.

	Masculine	*Feminine*
Singular	*ce* **train**	*cette* **valise**
Plural	*ces* **avions**	*ces* **photos**

Note also that **ce** will become **cet** and will be pronounced like **cette** in front of a masculine noun in the singular starting with a vowel or an **h**:

J'ai pris *cet* avion.
I took this/that plane.

In English, the demonstratives have two forms in the singular, 'this' and 'that', and two forms in the plural, 'these' and 'those'. The French do not normally make this distinction. When it is essential to contrast 'this' and 'that', they will add **-ci** or more likely **-là** and point to the thing/person they are talking about.

Vous voulez *cette table-là*?
Do you want that table?

Exercise 8

Fill in the blanks with **ce**, **cet**, **cette**, **ces**. If you are unsure of the gender of the nouns, check in your dictionary.

1 Avec _____billet, vous pouvez prendre _____ train.
2 _____ hôtel est très confortable.
3 _____ petite rue est vraiment adorable.
4 Tu aimes _____ chaussures? Elles sont hideuses!
5 Tu es allée à _____ réunion, _____ matin?

Exercise 9

Read the text and answer the questions.

La famille française a beaucoup évolué ces dernières années. Le format traditionnel du couple marié avec des enfants est bien sûr encore présent, même si les jeunes ont tendance à se marier plus tard dans leur vie. Ils veulent d'abord avoir un bon travail et profiter un peu de la vie de célibataire. On constate aussi que le nombre de familles monoparentales ou recomposées a beaucoup augmenté. Il est plus facile aujourd'hui de divorcer et de refaire sa vie. Et puis le concubinage n'est plus tabou. Enfin, beaucoup de jeunes choisissent aussi de ne pas habiter avec leur partenaire. Chacun a sa propre maison ou son propre appartement.

1 What is the traditional format?
2 Why do young people get married later in life?
3 What are the two types of family structure on the increase?
4 What are the two reasons given for such an increase?
5 And finally, what do a lot of young people choose to do?

In the descriptions below, pair each person with the type of relationship he/she has chosen.

6 le concubinage
7 la famille monoparentale
8 le format traditionnel
9 la famille recomposée
10 on choisit de ne pas habiter avec son partenaire

Maximilien

Ma copine et moi, nous voulons attendre un peu avant de vivre ensemble. J'ai 25 ans et elle 22 ans. On a du temps, quoi! J'ai mon appartement. Elle a son appartement. Et c'est très bien.

Je suis divorcée et j'ai un fils de 4 ans. Mais, je suis plus heureuse comme ça. Ça se passe très bien!

Cécile

J'ai 40 ans et j'habite avec Sarah depuis 15 ans. Se marier? Pour quoi faire? On est bien comme ça!

Matthieu

Je me suis marié à l'âge de 18 ans et j'ai 67 ans. Eh ben, je suis encore avec ma femme! C'est un excellent mariage!

Théo

J'ai divorcé de Pierre et j'ai épousé Jacques. Il a un fils de son premier mariage et moi une fille de 10 ans.

Hélène

9 On s'amuse bien

We are enjoying ourselves

> **In this unit you will learn about:**
>
> - using the **passé composé** with **être**
> - reflexive verbs
> - talking about something you have just done
> - using **ne . . . plus**, **ne . . . rien** and **ne . . . jamais**

Text 1

Anne is in Malika's flat and looking at two postcards that Malika received from friends on holiday. Can you spot the verbs in the **passé composé**? How many use **être**?

Chère Malika,

Nous sommes arrivés à Biarritz! Enfin, les vacances! Les enfants sont ravis. Ils sont partis à la plage et ils s'amusent bien. Marc et moi, nous nous reposons. On se lève tous les jours à 10 heures. Hier, nous nous sommes promenés en voiture le long de la côte. C'est magnifique!

Grosses bises,

Christine

Salut Malika!

Je suis à Périgueux. Dis-donc, on mange bien dans cette région! Hier soir, je suis resté dans un petit hôtel-restaurant et j'ai mangé du foie gras et du canard. Je me suis régalé. Demain, je pars à Cahors. Je vais voir mon amie Marina. Tu te souviens de Marina? Elle s'est mariée l'an dernier et elle est retournée vivre à Cahors. Et comme je ne suis jamais allé à Cahors...

Bises,

Philippe

Vocabulary

ravi	delighted	**la plage**	the beach
s'amuser	to have fun	**se reposer**	to rest
se lever	to get up	**se promener**	(*here*) to have/ to go for a walk
le long de	along	**la côte**	the coast
rester	to stay	**le canard**	duck
se régaler	to enjoy very much (normally of food)	**se souvenir de**	to remember
se marier	to get married	**comme**	as
ne ... jamais	never		

Biarritz

Foie gras

Language points

Using the passé composé *with verbs taking* être

With the following small group of verbs, you form the **passé composé** by combining the *present tense* of **être** with the *past participle* of the verb that you want to use.

Try memorising them in pairs of opposites. They are:

arriver, partir	to arrive, to leave
aller, venir	to go, to come
entrer, sortir	to come in, to go out
rester, passer	to stay, to pass by/call in
retourner	to go again/return
monter, descendre	to go up, to go down
naître, mourir	to be born, to die
tomber	to fall
devenir	to become
and compounds such as **rentrer**, **revenir**, and so on.	

Mes parents *sont venus* à Paris.

Elle *est tombée* de cheval.
She fell off her horse.

Il *est descendu* à Marseille.
He went down to Marseilles.

Tu *es né* à Paris?

Ils ne *sont* pas *sortis*.

Sandra n'*est* pas *devenue* journaliste.

Did you notice that the past participle agrees in gender and number with the subject in the same way as adjectives do?

Exercise 1

Look at the sentences below and say whether **je**, **tu** and **vous** represent a man or a woman.

1 Tu es parti très tôt.
2 Je suis retournée à Paris.
3 Vous êtes passé?
4 Tu es née en France?
5 Je suis venu, hier.
6 Vous êtes restée longtemps?

In which sentences below does **vous** represent a group of people? In which sentence does **vous** represent a group of women only?

7   Vous êtes arrivé!
8   Vous êtes sortis de Paris.
9   Vous êtes tombée.
10 Vous êtes restées au lit?
11 Vous êtes venus en voiture?

Exercise 2

Translate the following sentences into French.

1 Tim and Sandra went to the cinema.
2 He did not stay in bed.
3 She went back to Paris.
4 Anna became a journalist.
5 Malika and Anne stayed one night in a hotel.

Exercise 3

Bernard and Françoise went to Nice for a holiday last year. Using the vocabulary provided below, give an account of their stay.

arriver	Nice	10 juillet
rester	petit hôtel	
visiter	musées, monuments	
aller	Cannes, Saint-Tropez	
prendre	photos	
rentrer	Paris	22 juillet

Language points

Reflexive verbs

In French, a large number of verbs are reflexive. These verbs are made of a verb and a pronoun **se** which changes its form according to the subject of the verb. In our postcards we had seven reflexive verbs: **s'amuser** (to have fun), **se reposer** (to rest), **se lever** (to get up), **se promener** (to have/to go for a walk/a drive), **se régaler** (to enjoy/take a lot of pleasure), **se souvenir de** (to remember/recall), **se marier** (to get married).

Four of these verbs were used in the present tense. Can you spot them?

Ils *s'*amusent bien.
Nous *nous* reposons.
On *se* lève tous les jours à 10h.
Tu *te* souviens de Marina?

The verb se relaxer **(to relax)**

Je **me** relaxe	Nous **nous** relaxons
Tu **te** relaxes	Vous **vous** relaxez
Il/elle/on **se** relaxe	Ils/elles **se** relaxent

Note that **me, te** and **se** will drop the **e** if the verb starts with a vowel or an 'h'.

As **se** and its various forms are part of a reflexive verb, **ne ... pas** will be placed on each side of the block formed by **se** and the verb in the present tense.

> **Elle *ne* se repose *pas* beaucoup.**
> **Nous *ne* nous levons *pas* tard.**

Exercise 4

Put the verbs in brackets into the present tense.

1 Nous _____ (se lever) à 8 heures.
2 Il _____ (s'amuser) bien.
3 Vous _____ (se souvenir de) Pierre?
4 Je _____ (se reposer) devant la télévision.
5 Elles _____ (se promener) dans la ville.
6 Tu _____ (se marier) quand?

Exercise 5

Matthieu has won the lottery and his life has changed drastically. Make him talk, using the verbs below.

Je ...

> se lever à midi tous les jours
> se promener dans le parc
> se reposer
> s'occuper de ses enfants (to look after his children)
> s'amuser avec eux
> se coucher très tard (to go to bed very late)

Language points

Using reflexive verbs in the passé composé

Reflexive verbs take être in the passé composé

> **Nous nous sommes promenés en voiture.**
> **Je me suis régalé.**
> **Elle s'est mariée.**

As with our small group of verbs taking **être**, the past participles in our examples agree in gender and number with the subject of the verb. Though it is always the case with verbs such as **aller**, **venir**, etc., with reflexive verbs, it is not always so. You will learn more about this in Unit 11.

Ne ... pas is placed on each side of the pronoun and **être**.

Elle *ne* **s'est** *pas* **reposée.**
Vous *ne* **vous êtes** *pas* **amusé(e)(s)?**

Exercise 6

Can you tell when **je**, **tu** and **vous** represent a woman?

1 Je me suis couchée à minuit.
2 Tu t'es bien reposé?
3 Vous vous êtes amusée?
4 Je me suis promené le long de la côte.
5 Tu t'es levée à quelle heure?
6 Vous vous êtes marié à quel âge?

Exercise 7 (Audio 2; 6)

Give an account of Pierre's last holiday, using the verbs below.

Il ...

se lever à 11 heures tous les jours.

se promener sur la plage le matin.

se reposer l'après-midi.

ne pas se coucher tard.

s'ennuyer un peu. (to be/get a little bored)

Language points

Writing to people

Did you notice how Philippe and Christine started their card to Malika? In French, you can start a letter or a card to someone you know with **cher(s)**, **chère(s)** and the name of the person you are addressing. Among young people and friends who know each other very well, **salut** is frequently used.

Cher **Matthieu**
Chère **Sophie**

Chers **amis**
Chères **amies**

Salut **Max!**
Salut **Hélène.**

You can also use **cher(s)** and **chère(s)** with the surname of a person you know but are not friends with:

Cher **Monsieur Dumas**
Chère **Madame Leblanc**

When you do not know the person(s) you are writing to, you can either use **monsieur**, **madame** with their surname if you know it, or use **monsieur**, **madame** on their own.

To end a letter to someone you know, you have several options, depending on how well you know him/her. Here are a few:

amicalement *or* **amitiés**	best wishes
affectueusement	fondly
bises	love
je vous/t'embrasse *or* **grosses bises** *or* **bisous**	lots of love/hugs

Exercise 8

Imagine you are Malika and are writing a short postcard to Christine. Include the information below.

arriver à Marseille

se promener dans la ville

aller à la plage

se reposer

manger au restaurant

Dialogue 1 🎧 (Audio 2; 7)

Malika is listening to two messages left on her answerphone.

Allô Malika? C'est Julie. Je viens de rentrer du travail et j'ai eu ton message. Merci de ton invitation pour aller au cinéma, mais ce soir je ne peux pas. Marc vient manger. Il vient d'avoir les résultats de ses examens. Alors on va fêter ça! Le bonjour à Anne. Bisous. Salut!

Malika, c'est Thérèse, au travail. Je viens de taper cettre lettre pour Monsieur Dupré et je ne me souviens plus de son adresse. J'ai cherché dans votre carnet mais je n'ai rien trouvé. Vous pouvez me rappeler, s'il vous plaît? Merci. Au revoir.

Vocabulary

un résultat	a result	**des examens**	examinations
fêter	celebrate	**taper**	to type
un carnet	a (small) notebook	**rien**	nothing
rappeler	to call back		

Language points

Saying that you have just done something

When you want to say that you have just done something, you can use:

> present tense of **venir de** + verb in the infinitive

Je *viens de rentrer* du travail.
I've just come back from work.

Il *vient d'avoir* les résultats de ses examens.
He's just had the results of his exams.

Nous *venons de manger*.
We've just eaten.

Remember that outside the above structure **venir** means 'to come'. Compare:

Ils *viennent* de Marseille.
They come/are coming from Marseilles.

Vous *venez* jouer au tennis, ce soir?
Are you coming to play tennis tonight?

Vous *venez de* jouer au tennis?
Have you just played tennis?

Exercise 9

Translate the following sentences.

1 Malika is coming to England in July.
2 Are you coming to play golf on Sunday?
3 She's just arrived in Paris.
4 We've just watched a good film on TV.
5 They've just left.

Exercise 10 (Audio 2; 8)

Use the prompts in brackets to answer the following questions.

1 Tu veux venir au restaurant avec nous, ce soir? (no thanks, you've just eaten)
2 On va jouer au golf. Vous venez? (you're tired, you've just played tennis)
3 Allô, c'est Marie. Je peux parler à Annie? (sorry, she's just left)
4 On va faire de la marche en montagne. Tu veux venir? (you don't have time, you've just come back from holidays)

Language points

Did you notice?

Je *ne* me souviens *plus* de son adresse.
I can't remember his address any longer/more.

Ne ... plus is usually translated by 'any more', 'no more', 'any longer' or 'no longer' depending on the context.

Je *n'*ai *rien* trouvé.
I have found nothing.
or I didn't find/haven't found anything.

Je *ne* suis *jamais* allé à Cahors.
I have never been to Cahors.

Ne ... plus, **ne ... rien** and **ne ... jamais** will be placed in the same position as **ne ... pas**, on each side of the verb.

Exercise 11

Make sentences using the words given.

Example: **Ne / travaille / je / plus**
Je ne travaille plus.

1 Fait / il / rien / ne
2 Nous / au / plus / jouons / ne / golf
3 Ils / jamais / travaillent / ne
4 Trouvé / rien / n' / elles / ont
5 Vous / plus / n' / de / avez / monnaie
6 Elle / va / au / théâtre / ne / jamais

(Audio 2; 9)

Answer the questions in the negative, using **ne ... plus**, **ne ... rien** or **ne ... jamais**.

7 Vous allez souvent au théâtre à Paris?
    (say you no longer live in Paris)

8 On va manger au restaurant?
    (say you have no money left)

9 Il est à la retraite, non? Et il est toujours actif?
    (say yes, but he doesn't do anything)

10 Ils ont acheté une maison à Marseille?
    (say they haven't found anything)

11 Vous aimez le cinéma?
    (say you never go to the cinema)

12 Elle aime faire la cuisine?
    (say she never cooks)

10 A Paris

In Paris

In this unit you will learn about:

- expressing preferences and suggesting things to do
- using **y**
- talking about the weather
- saying where places are
- using **on**

Dialogue 1 🎧 (Audio 2; 10)

Visiter Paris

Malika and Anne are sitting on the terrace of a café in Paris. They are talking about what they are going to do in the afternoon.

MALIKA: On pourrait visiter le musée d'Orsay, cet après-midi. Ça te dit? Ou peut-être tu préférerais faire autre chose?

ANNE: Non, le musée d'Orsay, ça me tente. Je n'ai jamais vu une toile de Van Gogh en vrai. C'est une excellente idée.

MALIKA: Si tu aimes les musées, il y a le choix à Paris. Tu as déjà vu le Louvre. Mais est-ce que tu es allée au musée de Cluny pour voir la *Dame à la Licorne*? C'est superbe. J'y vais une fois par an.

ANNE: Non, je n'y suis jamais allée. Mais comme il fait beau, j'aimerais mieux me promener sur les bords de la Seine. Et puis, on pourrait manger dans le Quartier Latin.

MALIKA: Bonne idée. C'est vrai, on a de la chance en ce
            moment. Il n'a pas plu de toute la semaine. Et puis,
            j'aime bien me balader sur les bords de la Seine. Ma
            mère et moi, nous y allons souvent quand elle vient
            à Paris.
ANNE: Alors, tu as fini ton café? Tu es prête? On y va?

Vocabulary

autre chose	something else	**une toile**	a painting
en vrai	(literally) in real	**il y a le choix**	(*here*) (you are) spoilt for choice
une licorne	a unicorn	**on a de la chance**	we are lucky
pleuvoir	to rain (past participle **plu**)	**se balader**	(*here*) to go for a stroll
se promener	to go for a walk	**les bords**	(*here*) the banks

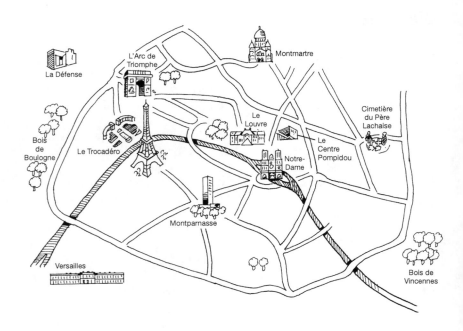

Language points

Expressing preferences

To say what you would prefer or would rather have or do, you can use:

Je *préférerais* aller au musée du Louvre.
I'd rather go to the Louvre.

Je *préférerais* un café.
I'd rather have a coffee.

J'*aimerais mieux* me promener dans les rues.
I'd rather walk in the streets.

J'*aimerais mieux* une glace au chocolat.
I'd rather have a chocolate ice cream.

As you can see, both can be followed by a noun or another verb in the infinitive.

To ask about what someone would like to have or to do, you can use:

    Ça te dit?
or
    Ça te tente?

Both can be translated as 'How about that?', 'Would you like that/to do that?'.

Did you notice?

Both Malika and Anne made suggestions of things they could do in Paris. They used a verb that you have already come across in Unit 7, **pouvoir**. Here, **pouvoir** is in the same form as **aimer** and **préférer** above. This form is called the conditional and you will learn more about it in future units.

On *pourrait* visiter le musée d'Orsay.
We could visit the Orsay museum.

On *pourrait* manger dans le Quartier Latin.
We could eat in the Latin Quarter.

Exercise 1 🎧 (Audio 2; 11)

Using the form of **pouvoir** you have just learned and the vocabulary provided, make suggestions.

> *Example*: **manger au restaurant**
> **On pourrait manger au restaurant.**

1 sortir prendre un verre
2 aller au cinéma
3 partir en week-end
4 se reposer
5 se promener dans Montmartre

Exercise 2 🎧 (Audio 2; 12)

Now respond to the following suggestions by saying what you'd rather do, following the example.

> *Example*: **On pourrait sortir prendre un verre.**
> **(aller au restaurant)**
> **Je** *préférerais/j'aimerais mieux* **aller au restaurant.**

1 On pourrait aller au musée du Louvre.   (visiter le musée de Cluny)
2 On pourrait partir en week-end.   (se reposer)
3 On pourrait faire les magasins.   (regarder la télévision)
4 On pourrait louer un camping-car.   (aller à l'hôtel)
5 On pourrait se marier.   (rester célibataire)

Language points

Using y

The pronoun **y** can be used to replace phrases expressing *a place* and beginning with prepositions such as **à**, **dans**, **sur**, **devant**, **derrière**, **chez**. Pronouns such as **y** are always placed *before the verb* to which they relate.

> **Mais est-ce que tu es déjà allée** *au musée de Cluny* **pour voir la** *Dame à la Licorne*? **J'y vais une fois par an.**
> But have you already been to the Cluny museum to see the *Dame à la Licorne*? I go there once a year.

Et puis, j'aime bien me balader *sur les bords de la Seine*. Ma mère et moi, nous *y* allons souvent quand elle vient à Paris.
And I like to walk along the banks of the Seine. My mother and I often go there when she comes to Paris.

Combien de temps est-ce qu'elle est restée *à Paris*?
Elle *y* est restée trois jours, je crois.

Whereas it is often possible in English to omit the pronoun 'there', in French **y** is normally always present.
When used in a negative sentence, the **ne** comes in front of **y**.

J'ai cherché ces clés *dans toute la maison* et elles *n'y* sont *pas*.
I've searched the whole house for those keys and they are not here.

Tu es allée au musée de Cluny?
Non, je *n'y* suis *jamais* allée.

y is also used in phrases such as:

On y va?	**On y va.**
Shall we go?	We're off.
Vas-y! *or* **Allez-y!**	**Allons-y!**
Go on!	Let's go.

Exercise 3

Answer the following questions using **y** and making complete sentences.

    Example: **Vous allez à Paris dimanche?**
                Oui, j'y vais dimanche.

1 Vous restez à l'hôtel deux nuits?
2 Elles vont au cinéma avec des amis?
3 Vous êtes allé(e) en France l'an dernier?
4 Les clés sont sur la table?
5 Ils sont allés au restaurant?

Now, answer the same questions in the negative using **y** and making complete sentences.

    Example: **Vous allez à Paris dimanche?**
                Non, je n'y vais pas dimanche.

Language points

Talking about the weather

You can use the following expressions to talk about the weather.
In all cases, **il** cannot be replaced by any other word.

Il fait beau.	It's fine/sunny.
Il fait gris.	It's cloudy.
Il fait chaud.	It's hot.
Il fait froid.	It's cold.
Il fait bon.	It's warm/pleasant.
Il pleut.	It's raining.
Il neige.	It's snowing. (infinitive **neiger**)
Il y a du soleil.	It's sunny.
Il y a du vent.	It's windy.
Il y a de la pluie.	It's raining.
Il y a du brouillard.	It's foggy.
Il y a de l'orage.	It's stormy.

You can use **il fait ...** to say:

Il fait jour.	It's daylight.
Il fait nuit.	It's night/dark [because it's night].
Il fait noir.	It's dark/pitch black [either because it's night or because you're in a dark place].

Exercise 4

Tell a friend what the weather is like today and what it was like
yesterday.

> Aujourd'hui: soleil, vent.
> Temperature maximale: 15 degrés Celsius
>
> Hier: pluie et neige.
> Température maximale: 2 degrés Celsius.

Dialogue 2 🎧 (Audio 2; 13)

Où est-ce que ça se trouve?

Malika and Anne are having a meal in the Quartier Latin, not far from Notre-Dame. Malika is telling Anne about places of interest in Paris.

MALIKA: Tu connais Montmartre?

ANNE: C'est un quartier de Paris non?

MALIKA: Oui, c'est un quartier qui se trouve au nord. C'est très touristique. Il y a le Sacré-Cœur évidemment, mais aussi toutes les petites rues et les escaliers où on peut se promener des heures et des heures.

ANNE: Hier, tu as parlé de Montparnasse.

MALIKA: Ah oui, c'est un autre quartier de Paris. C'est le quartier des intellectuels. C'est situé au sud. C'est célèbre aussi à cause de la Tour Montparnasse qui fait 210 mètres de haut.

ANNE: Et on peut monter tout en haut?

MALIKA: Oui, oui, bien sûr. Il y a un restaurant panoramique au 56ᵉ étage. On y mange très bien et puis on voit tout Paris.

ANNE: J'aimerais bien y aller la prochaine fois.

MALIKA: Bien sûr. Mais la prochaine fois, on va aussi voir le Centre Pompidou et se promener dans le quartier du Marais.

Vocabulary

un quartier	an area	**se trouver**	to be found, situated
c'est situé	it's situated	**le nord**	the north
le sud	the south	**les escaliers**	the stairs
à cause de	because of	**en haut**	at the top

Language points

Saying where places are

To say where places are, you can use the following expressions:

Montmartre *est au nord du* centre.
Montmartre is north of the centre.

La tour Montparnasse *est située au sud du* **centre.**
The Montparnasse Tower is situated south of the centre.

La tour Eiffel *se trouve à l'ouest du* **centre.**
The Eiffel Tower is situated west of the centre.

Le bois de Vincennes? *C'est situé au sud-est de* **Paris.**
The Bois de Vincennes? It's situated south east of Paris.

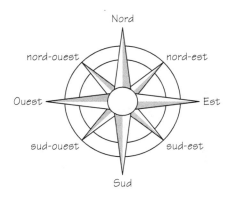

You can also use:

Versailles?
   C'est **un château** *qui est situé* **au sud-ouest de Paris.**
   It's a castle which is situated south west of Paris.

Orly?
   C'est **un aéroport** *qui se trouve* **au sud de Paris.**
   It's an airport which is situated south of Paris.

Exercise 5

Using the map on p. 124, say where the following places are.

  Example: **Montmartre**
                Montmarte est/est situé/se trouve au nord du centre.

1 Montparnasse
2 Versailles
3 Le bois de Boulogne
4 Le quartier de la Défense
5 L'Arc de Triomphe
6 Le cimetière du Père Lachaise

Exercise 6 🎧 (Audio 2; 14)

Now make sentences following the example.

Example: **Montmartre   quartier**
           **Montmartre, c'est un quartier qui est situé/
           se trouve au nord.**

le Sacré-Cœur   une basilique
la Défense   un quartier
Versailles   un château
le Louvre   un musée
le Centre Pompidou   un bâtiment moderne

Language points

Using on

You have already encountered in Unit 5 the pronoun **on**, which is
frequently used instead of **nous**.

La prochaine fois, *on* va aussi voir le Centre Pompidou.
Next time, we're going to see the Pompidou Centre, too.

On can also be used to talk about someone or people in general
who remain unidentified. In these cases, it can be generally be translated by *one* or *you* (meaning anyone). Look at Dialogue 2 again.

... les escaliers où *on* peut se promener ...
where one/you can stroll

Et *on* peut monter tout en haut?
And one/you can go right to the top?

***On* y mange très bien et *on* voit tout Paris.**
The food is very good and all of Paris can be seen from there.

Exercise 7

Explain to a friend what your home town offers to tourists, using
on and the vocabulary provided below.

Example: **visiter le château**
           On peut visiter le château.

monter en haut de la tour
voir toute la ville
se balader dans les petites rues
manger très bien dans les restaurants indiens
aller boire des bières traditionnelles dans les pubs.

Exercise 8

Read the text 'Montmartre' and underline the parts of the text that
answer the questions that follow it.

Montmartre

Montmartre reste un des quartiers les plus visités de Paris. Il
est situé au nord du centre, et le touriste y trouve tout le
charme du vieux Paris.

La basilique du Sacré-Cœur avec sa façade blanche est
caractéristique du goût du 19ᵉ siècle pour l'éclectisme. On y
trouve de superbes mosaïques. Le dôme offre un remarquable
panorama sur Paris.

Autour du Sacré-Cœur, on peut se balader des heures et
des heures dans les petites rues pittoresques et les escaliers.
C'est le Paris romantique et désuet des cartes postales et des
photographes célèbres comme Doisneau, par exemple.

La place du Tertre, ancienne place villageoise, accueille les
touristes qui veulent se reposer aux multiples terrasses de café
et aussi les chevalets des peintres qui cherchent à faire
fortune. C'est ici que le mot russe 'bistro' ('vite') a fait son

apparition, amené par les occupants russes au début du 19ᵉ siècle. Au nord de la place du Tertre, la rue Saint-Rustique a neuf siècles et a conservé ses pavés et son caniveau central.

Vocabulary

l'éclectisme	eclecticism	**désuet**	old fashioned
une carte postale	a postcard	**accueillir**	to welcome
un chevalet	an easel	**un caniveau**	a gutter

1 Why is Montmartre so popular with tourists?
2 What can you see from the dome of the Sacré-Cœur?
3 What can you do around the Sacré-Cœur?
4 What attractions can you find on the place du Tertre?
5 Where does the word 'bistro' come from?
6 How old is the rue Saint-Rustique and what's special about it?

Le Sacré-Cœur

11 Problèmes de santé

Health problems

In this unit you will learn about:

- more reflexive verbs
- talking about injuries or health problems
- using **depuis**
- giving advice
- using the imperative

Dialogue 1 (Audio 2; 15)

Jacques a des problèmes

Jacques, whom you met in Unit 4, is not feeling too well and talks to a work colleague who tries to give him some advice.

PAUL: Ça ne va pas, aujourd'hui?
JACQUES: Ça va, ça va.
PAUL: Pourtant, tu n'as pas l'air en forme.
JACQUES: Ben, j'ai mal à la tête depuis trois jours et je suis très fatigué. Je dors très mal aussi. La nuit dernière je me suis réveillé au moins cinq fois. Alors, tu comprends, quand je me lève, c'est pas la forme!
PAUL: Et tu te couches tard?
JACQUES: Non. Nous nous couchons de bonne heure. Je m'endors très vite. C'est pas comme ma femme, d'ailleurs! Elle met un temps fou à s'endormir.
PAUL: Tu es peut-être un peu stressé en ce moment. Tu devrais te reposer ou prendre des vacances.

JACQUES: En ce moment c'est impossible. J'ai quelques pro-
           blèmes avec un client et ma femme s'inquiète pour la
           santé de son père. Il a des problèmes de cœur. On ne
           sait pas exactement quoi encore. Il n'est pas bien
           depuis quelques mois, maintenant et ma femme passe
           beaucoup de temps avec lui.
PAUL: Ah oui, c'est difficile quand un membre de ta famille
           n'est pas en bonne santé.
JACQUES: Toi, par contre, tu as l'air en forme.
PAUL: Ah oui! Je me suis pesé ce matin et j'ai encore perdu
           un kilo!
JACQUES: Tu fais un régime?
PAUL: Oui, et en plus je fais de l'exercice trois fois par
           semaine depuis six mois. Je me sens en pleine forme.
           Tu devrais essayer.

Vocabulary

avoir l'air	to seem/look (unwell for example)	**avoir mal à la tête**	to have a headache
dormir	to sleep	**en forme**	well, in good health
se réveiller	to wake up	**s'endormir**	to fall asleep, to go to sleep
se coucher	to go to bed	**se lever**	to get up
s'inquiéter	to worry	**se peser**	to weigh oneself
se sentir bien/ en pleine forme	to feel well/ on top form	**mettre du temps**	to take time
un régime	a diet	**essayer**	to try

Language points

Talking about your general health

To ask how people are, you can use:

Vous allez bien?
Are you well?

Comment allez-vous?
How are you?

Ça va?
How are you?

To say how you are, you can use:

Je vais bien.   **Ça va (très) bien.**
I'm well.   I'm (very) well.

Je suis en (pleine) forme.   **Je me sens en (pleine) forme.**
I'm (very) well.   I'm (very) well.

Ça ne va pas (très) bien.   **Je ne me sens pas (très) bien.**
I don't feel well/very well.   I don't feel (very) well.

Ce n'est pas la forme. C'est pas la forme.
I'm not on top form.

You can also use the following to describe what is wrong with you:

Je suis	**fatigué(e)**	tired
	épuisé(e)	exhausted
	crevé(e)	shattered (familiar)
	stressé(e)	stressed
	énervé(e)	irritated, edgy
J'ai des problèmes	**de cœur**	heart
	d'estomac	stomach
	de dents	teeth
	de poids	weight
	de digestion	digestion
	de vue	eyesight
	de tension	blood pressure

Did you notice?

Jacques and Paul used the same expression:

Tu n'as pas *l'air* en forme.   Tu *as l'air* en forme.
You don't look well.   You look well.

You can use **avoir l'air** in a lot of contexts and generally with adjectives:

Vous *avez l'air* contrarié.
You look annoyed.

Il *a l'air* crevé.
He looks shattered. (informal 'tired')

Tu *as l'air* malade.
You look ill.

Exercise 1

Following the example and using **avoir l'air** and the vocabulary provided, comment on the following people.

> *Example*: **Michel vient de faire 20 km en vélo.**
> **Il a l'air épuisé.**

1 Christine a perdu 3 kilos en deux mois et va régulièrement à la piscine.
2 Paul vient de gagner 3000 euros à la Loterie.
3 Marc a beaucoup de problèmes avec un de ses clients. Il ne dort pas la nuit.
4 Sandra et Bernard ont trouvé des cafards (cockroaches) dans leur chambre d'hôtel.

---

en colère   heureux   en pleine forme   stressé

Language points

Further reflexive verbs

In Unit 9, you encountered some reflexive verbs. In Dialogue 1 of this unit, you were introduced to some more. Spot how many are used by Paul and Jacques.

La nuit dernière je *me suis réveillé* au moins cinq fois.
Last night I woke up at least five times.

Quand *je me lève*, c'est pas la forme!
When I get up, I don't feel too great!

Tu *te couches* tard?
Do you go to bed late?

Je *m'endors* très vite.
I fall asleep very quickly.

Ma femme _s'inquiète_ pour la santé de son père.
My wife is worried about her father's health.

Je _me suis pesé_ ce matin.
I weighed myself this morning.

Je _me sens_ en pleine forme.
I feel in top form/great.

Here are some other useful reflexive verbs:

se raser	to shave
se maquiller	to put on make-up
se doucher	to shower
s'habiller	to get dressed
se coiffer	to do one's hair

Exercise 2

Using as many reflexive verbs as possible, imagine what these people do, what time they get up, go to bed, and so on.

Example: **Il/elle se lève à 8 heures. Il/elle se rase/se maquille etc. ...**

la Reine d'Angleterre
Batman
Bill Gates
Elizabeth Hurley (actress and model)

Exercise 3 (Audio 2; 17)

What time do you normally get up at during the week? What time do you normally go to bed at? What about last weekend? Answer the questions in French using reflexive verbs.

Language points

Giving advice

To give advice, you can use:

Tu _devrais_ te reposer.
You should rest.

Tu *devrais* **essayer.**
You should try.

Vous *devriez* **manger moins.**
You should eat less.

The verb used above is **devoir**, here in the conditional. You simply need to know how to use these two forms for now. You will learn more about the conditional in Unit 13.

Exercise 4 (Audio 2; 18)

Respond to the following people, giving advice and using the forms of **devoir** you have just learned.

Example: **Je suis stressé, en ce moment.**
              Tu devrais te reposer/vous devriez vous reposer.

1 J'ai encore pris 1 kilo!
2 Je suis crevé.
3 Je viens de gagner un million à la Loterie!
4 J'ai des problèmes d'estomac.

Language points

Using depuis

To say 'since when' or 'how long for' something has been going on, you can use **depuis**.

J'*ai* **mal à la tête** *depuis* **trois jours.**
I've had a headache *for* three days.

Je *fais* **de l'exercice trois fois par semaine** *depuis* **six mois.**
I have been exercising three times a week *for* six months.

Il *habite* **en France** *depuis* **janvier 2004.**
He has been living in France *since* January 2004.

Be careful!

Depuis is normally used with the present tense. This is because the action/event is viewed as still ongoing.

Exercise 5

Translate the following sentences.

1 He has been working in France for seven years.
2 She has been looking after the children since last week.
3 They have been on holiday for two weeks now.
4 He's been working with them since Christmas.

Dialogue 2 🎧 (Audio 2; 19)

Chez le docteur

Jacques is not better and decides to visit the doctor for a second time.

DOCTEUR:	Bonjour. Ça ne va pas mieux?
JACQUES:	Ben, docteur, ce n'est pas la grosse forme. Je ne dors toujours pas et je suis très fatigué. Et en plus, la semaine dernière, je suis tombé et je me suis fait mal à la cheville.
DOCTEUR:	Vous avez encore mal?
JACQUES:	Oui, ça va un petit peu mieux mais c'est encore un peu douloureux.
DOCTEUR:	Voyons. Je vais regarder. Oui, c'est un peu enflé. Bougez le pied et les orteils. Vous avez mal quand j'appuie là?
JACQUES:	Un peu.
DOCTEUR:	Bon, c'est pas bien grave. Vous vous êtes foulé la cheville. Evitez de marcher trop dans les jours qui suivent. Ça devrait aller mieux dans deux ou trois jours.
JACQUES:	Et pour mes insomnies, docteur?
DOCTEUR:	Vous avez suivi mes conseils? Vous faites un peu d'exercice, maintenant? Vous devriez aussi essayer la relaxation. Ça donne d'excellents résultats.
JACQUES:	Je suis allé à la piscine, mais vous savez avec le travail, c'est pas facile.
DOCTEUR:	Bon, mais continuez quand même. Je vais vous prescrire des somnifères légers, mais juste pour une semaine. Revenez dans quinze jours, si ça ne va pas mieux.

Vocabulary

se faire mal à la cheville	to hurt one's ankle	**avoir mal**	to be in pain
douloureux	painful	**mieux**	better
enflé	swollen	**bouger**	to move
le pied	the foot	**un orteil**	a toe
appuyer	to press	**grave**	serious
se fouler la cheville	to sprain one's ankle	**éviter**	to avoid
suivre	to follow	**prescrire**	to prescribe
des somnifères	sleeping tablets		

Language points

Talking about pains and injuries

To talk about pain in parts of your body, you can say:

J'ai mal	**à la tête**	I have a headache
	aux dents	I have a toothache
	au ventre	... stomach/tummy
	aux jambes	... legs
	au dos	... back
	au bras	... arm

To say that you've hurt a part of your body, you can say:

Je me suis fait mal	**au bras**	I've hurt/hurt my	arm
	au dos		back
	au poignet		wrist
	au genou		knee
	à l'épaule		shoulder

You can also talk about specific injuries like this:

Sylvia s'est cassé **le bras.**
Sylvia broke/has broken her arm.

Elle s'est foulé **la cheville.**
She sprained/has sprained her ankle.

Je me suis brûlé **le doigt.**
I burned/have burned my finger.

Il s'est coupé **au doigt.**
He cut/has cut his finger.

Did you notice?

All the verbs used above to talk about injuries are reflexive verbs. As you saw in Unit 9, when they are used in the **passé composé**, they usually agree in gender and number with the subject of the verb. Here, this is not the case.

Sylvia s'est cassé **le bras.**

Elle s'est foulé **la cheville.**

This is because the verbs are followed by a direct object: **le bras**, **la cheville**.

It's not always easy for an English speaker to recognise a direct object. But the French occasionally have difficulties, too!

The simplest way is to see if the subject and the verb are followed by something that answers the question **quoi** (what) or **qui** (who (m)):

Sylvia s'est cassé *quoi*?   **le bras**
Sylvia has broken/broke *what*?

Elle s'est foulé *quoi*?   **la cheville**
She has sprained/sprained *what*?

Bernard a vu son docteur.
Bernard a vu *qui*?   **son docteur**
Bernard saw *who(m)*?

You will learn more about direct objects in later units.

Minor ailments and symptoms

J'ai la grippe.   **Elle *a un rhume*.**
I have the flu.   She's got a cold.

J'ai de la fièvre.   **Elle *a une indigestion*.**
I have a temperature.   She's got indigestion.

Exercise 6

Match the statements on the left with the logical result on the right.

1 Je me suis cassé la jambe.   (a) Il ne peut pas écrire.
2 J'ai mal à la tête.   (b) Elle ne peut pas jouer au
                                         golf.
3 Il s'est brûlé à la main droite.   (c) Il ne peut rien manger.
4 Elle s'est fait mal au dos.   (d) Je ne peux pas conduire.
5 Il a très mal aux dents.   (e) Je suis au lit depuis une
                                         semaine.
6 J'ai la grippe.   (f) Je n'ai pas les idées
                                         claires.

Language points

Giving instructions

To give instructions you can use the imperative form of a verb:

Bougez le pied et les orteils.
Move your foot and toes.

Evitez de marcher trop.
Avoid walking too much.

Continuez quand même.
Keep at it, still.

Revenez **dans quinze jours, si ça ne va pas mieux.**
Come back in a fortnight, if it's not better.

Ne *marchez* **pas sur l'herbe.**
Don't walk on the grass.

With relexive verbs, the reflexive form of the pronoun (**se**) is placed after the verb:

Levez-vous!   **Couchez-vous de bonne heure.**
Get up!   Go to bed early.

To form the imperative, you simply remove the subject pronoun (**vous**, **tu**, **nous**) and use the verb in its present-tense form. Note that with most **-er verbs**, there will no **-s** in the **tu** form.

Regarde!   Look!

(**tu** form: you are addressing someone that you know very well)

Regardez!   Look!

(**vous** form: you are addressing a group of people or a person that you don't well enough to address with the **tu** form)

Regardons!   Let's have a look!

In this unit, you will only practise the **vous** form of the imperative. You will learn more in Unit 14.

Exercise 7 🎧 (Audio 2; 20)

Christian is at the doctor's explaining what's wrong with him. Take the role of the doctor and give Christian instructions, using the imperative form of the verbs provided.

1 CHRISTIAN: Je suis très fatigué.
   DOCTEUR: _____ de bonne heure.
2 CHRISTIAN: Je dors très mal.
   DOCTEUR: _____ un peu d'exercice.
3 CHRISTIAN: Je fais du tennis et je vais à la piscine.
   DOCTEUR: _____ en vacances.
4 CHRISTIAN: Je ne peux pas. J'ai trop de travail.
   DOCTEUR: _____ ces somnifères. Si ça ne va pas mieux
   _____ dans une semaine.

| partir | revenir | se coucher | faire | prendre |

Cultural point

You will not normally have to make an appointment if you need to consult **un généraliste** (GP). Until recently, visits to a doctor in France were normally charged directly to the patient. The French then claimed part, most or all of their money back from the **Sécurité Sociale and Mutuelles** (additional insurance cover). If given **une ordonnance** (a prescription) they would normally also need to pay for their medicines and claim part, most or all of their money back in the same way. Now, the introduction of an electronic card, **la Carte Vitale**, allows patients to be charged only for the difference not covered by their insurance, the doctor and chemist being paid directly by the **Sécurité Sociale** and relevant **Mutuelles**.

12 Souvenirs

Memories

In this unit you will learn about:

- using the **imparfait** (imperfect)
- using **parce que** and **à cause de**
- comparing things

Dialogue 1 🎧 (Audio 2; 21)

Nos toutes premières vacances

Jacques and Chantal are going away for the weekend. We pick up their conversation as they are driving in rather bad weather conditions.

CHANTAL:	Il y a vraiment beaucoup de brouillard. On pourrait peut-être s'arrêter dans un hôtel.
JACQUES:	Je voudrais continuer un petit peu. Il n'est que 6 heures. On a le temps, non?
CHANTAL:	Je ne me sens pas très rassurée avec tout ce brouillard. La visibilité est presque nulle.
JACQUES:	Ne t'inquiète pas. Je suis très prudent.
CHANTAL:	Tu te souviens de nos premières vacances?
JACQUES:	Quand on est parti en Bourgogne dans la vieille Renault® de ton père? Tu parles de vacances! C'était plutôt raté. Bah, on était jeune, tiens!
CHANTAL:	Ben, on avait 22 ans. C'était en décembre et c'était nos toutes premières vacances. Il ne faisait vraiment pas beau, mais on voulait partir quand même.

JACQUES: Je me souviens surtout de la voiture de ton père. La radio et le chauffage ne marchaient pas, le coffre ne fermait pas bien et il pleuvait à l'intérieur. J'oublie quelque chose?

CHANTAL: C'était un peu folklorique! Mais, on n'avait pas encore assez d'argent pour acheter une voiture.

JACQUES: Je me rappelle aussi ce camion devant nous. Je ne pouvais pas doubler parce qu'il roulait assez vite. Et à cause de la pluie, je ne voyais pas grand-chose.

CHANTAL: Oui, et tout à coup le pare-brise a éclaté. J'ai eu une de ces peurs!

JACQUES: C'était le début et la fin de nos premières vacances.

Vocabulary

le brouillard	fog	**s'arrêter**	to stop
rassuré	reassured, comfortable	**nul/nulle**	non-existent, nil
s'inquiéter	to worry	**tu parles de vacances!**	talk about a holiday (ironic comment)
raté	failed, spoilt, messed-up	**le chauffage**	heating
marcher	to function/work	**le coffre**	the boot
fermer	to close, shut	**quelque chose**	something

folklorique	outlandish	**se rappeler**	to remember
un camion	a lorry	**doubler**	to overtake
rouler	to go (of a wheeled vehicle)	**la pluie**	rain
voir	to see	**tout à coup**	suddenly
le pare-brise	the windscreen	**éclater**	to shatter
avoir peur	to be scared	**la fin**	the end

Language points

Talking about the past with the imparfait

The **imparfait** (imperfect) is easy to form. You take the **nous** form of the verb in the *present tense*, remove the ending **-ons** and use what's left as the stem. You then add the endings of the **imparfait** (**-ais, -ais, -ait, -ions, -iez, -aient**) to the stem as shown:

aller   →   **nous allons**   →   stem: **all-**

j'all*ais*
tu all*ais*
il/elle/on all*ait*
nous all*ions*
vous all*iez*
ils/elles all*aient*

This pattern works for all verbs apart from one, **être** which uses **ét-** as the stem.

Nous *étions* en vacances.

The **imparfait** is also easy to pronounce since four of the six forms (**je, tu, il/elle/on, ils/elles**) are pronounced in exactly the same way.

You have already come across one tense (the **passé composé**) to talk about the past.

Tout à coup le pare-brise *a éclaté*.
Suddenly, the windscreen shattered.

The **imparfait** can generally be translated in three ways but here too, relying on translation might prove very treacherous.

Je *jouais* au tennis.
I used to play tennis.
or   I was playing tennis.
or   I played tennis.

Use the **imparfait** when you are talking about something which is *descriptive* or provides *a background* to key events told in the **passé composé**.

                          1   2
Je regardais le match de football quand *il est arrivé*.
I was watching the football match when he arrived.

where (1) is the background information and (2) is the key event.

Uses of the **imparfait** can include:

• what the weather was like:

   Il ne *faisait* vraiment pas beau.
   The weather really wasn't good.

• when or where it was:

   C'était en décembre.   **On *était* à Paris.**
   It was in December.   We were in Paris.

• the characteristics of someone or something:

   Il *était* grand.   **On *avait* 22 ans.**
   He was tall.   We were 22 years old.

   La radio et le chauffage ne *marchaient* pas, le coffre ne *fermait* pas bien.
   The radio and the heating didn't work and the boot didn't shut properly.

• the description of the setting or what was taking place at the time:

   Je ne *pouvais* pas doubler parce qu'il *roulait* assez vite.
   I couldn't overtake because he was going quite fast.

Exercise 1 (Audio 2; 22)

Put the verbs in brackets in the **imparfait**.

1 Nous _____ (venir) de manger.
2 Il _____ (partir) en vacances.

3 Tu _____ (faire) la vaisselle?
4 Elles _____ (devoir) travailler.
5 J' _____ (avoir) 35 ans.
6 On _____ (pouvoir) sortir tous les soirs.
7 Vous _____ (vouloir) devenir actrice?
8 Nous _____ (être) fatigués.

Exercise 2

Should it be the **imparfait** or the **passé composé**? Put the verbs in brackets in the correct form.

> C' _____ (1 être) en juin. Nous _____ (2 rentrer) de vacances, ma femme et moi. Nous _____ (3 rouler) sur une petite route de campagne. Il _____ (4 être) tard et il _____ (5 commencer) à faire nuit. Tout d'un coup, nous _____ (6 voir) quelque chose traverser la route, juste devant notre voiture. Nous _____ (7 s'arrêter) et nous _____ (8 descendre) de la voiture pour regarder. Juste au bord de la route, il y _____ (9 avoir) un renard et il _____ (10 regarder) ma femme et moi avec surprise, sans bouger. Ma femme _____ (11 dire) quelque chose et le renard _____ (12 s'enfuir).

Vocabulary

une route	a road
un renard	a fox
s'enfuir	to flee/escape (past participle **enfui**)

Exercise 3 🎧 (Audio 2; 23)

Read Dialogue 1 again. Using the clues below, retell Jacques and Chantal's first holiday.

> C'était en décembre. Jacques et Chantal avaient 22 ans. Ils partaient en Bourgogne avec la voiture des parents de Chantal ...

faire vraiment pas beau
la radio et le chauffage
marcher
le coffre
fermer

pleuvoir à l'intérieur
avoir un camion devant eux
pas pouvoir doubler
rouler assez vite
le pare-brise éclater

Language points

Expressing the cause of something

To introduce a cause, you can use **parce que** and **à cause de**. **Parce que** is always followed by a *clause* (subject + verb).

Je ne pouvais pas doubler *parce qu'*il roulait assez vite.
I couldn't overtake because he was going quite fast.

Parce que is also closely linked with the question **pourquoi**.

Pourquoi **est-ce qu'il n'est pas là?**
*Parce qu'*il est malade.

A cause de is normally followed by a *noun* or a *pronoun*.

Et *à cause de* **la pluie, je ne voyais pas grand-chose.**
And because of the rain, I couldn't see much.

Exercise 4

Link the following facts with the corresponding cause, using **parce que** or **à cause de**.

Il est resté au lit toute la journée	il avait un rendez-vous chez un client
La route est fermée	le brouillard
Il est parti de bonne heure	il ne se sentait pas bien
Il ne voyait pas grand-chose	un accident

Did you notice?

In French, two verbs can be translated by 'to remember'. They are **se souvenir de** and **se rappeler**.

Tu *te souviens de* nos premières vacances?
Do you remember our first holiday?

Je *me rappelle* aussi ce camion devant nous.
I also remember/recall that lorry in front of us.

Dialogue 2 ⌒ (Audio 2; 24)

De bons souvenirs

*Jacques and Chantal are in their hotel room, watching Albert Coste
being interviewed on television.*

JOURNALISTE:	Vous êtes né en 1925. Vous avez donc 80 ans aujourd'hui. Quels sont vos souvenirs d'enfance?
ALBERT:	Nous habitions à la campagne. Mon père était agriculteur. Il n'y avait pas encore beaucoup de voitures à l'époque. On se déplaçait moins facilement. Mes frères et moi allions à l'école à pied. On faisait bien 5 kilomètres par jour pour aller au village. La vie était peut-être plus dure par certains côtés, mais on vivait mieux qu'aujourd'hui. On prenait plus de temps pour faire les choses. Evidemment, mes parents avaient moins d'argent, mais on était heureux.
JOURNALISTE:	Vous vous souvenez de la deuxième guerre mondiale?
ALBERT:	Oui. Mon père est entré dans la Résistance. Mes frères étaient fascinés. Moi, j'étais le plus jeune, je ne comprenais pas grand-chose. J'avais juste 15 ans et je m'intéressais plus aux filles qu'à la guerre.
JOURNALISTE:	Quel est votre meilleur souvenir?
ALBERT:	La naissance de ma fille. J'étais à l'étranger pour affaires. Je présentais un projet à des clients potentiels. Tout se passait très bien et puis j'ai eu la nouvelle de la naissance de ma fille en pleine réunion. J'étais tellement heureux, je n'arrivais plus à parler! J'ai expliqué pourquoi à tous ces hommes d'affaires et ils ont ri. Quand je suis retourné à mon hôtel, le soir, il y avait une bouteille de champagne sur la table dans ma chambre avec une carte de

félicitations de leur part. J'ai bu toute la bouteille dans la soirée. Je n'avais jamais bu autant de champagne!

Vocabulary

un souvenir	a memory	**l'enfance**	childhood
la campagne	the countryside	**un agriculteur**	a farmer
à l'époque	in those days	**se déplacer**	to move, to travel
dur	hard	**par certains côtés**	in some ways
mieux	better	**une guerre mondiale**	a world war
s'intéresser à	to get/be interested in	**une fille**	a girl
meilleur	best	**la naissance**	the birth
à l'étranger	abroad	**pour affaires**	on business
se passer bien	to go well	**la nouvelle**	the news
une réunion	a meeting	**tellement heureux**	so happy
arriver à	to manage (to do something)	**rire**	to laugh (past participle: **ri**)
félicitations	congratulations	**de leur part**	from them
Je n'avais jamais bu autant de champagne	I had never drunk so much champagne		

Language points

Comparing with plus, moins, aussi

You learned how to compare things by using **plus**, **moins** and **aussi** with *adjectives*:

> **La vie était peut-être *plus dure* par certains côtés.**
> Life was maybe harder in some ways.

The only exception concerns **bon**:

> **Ton plat est *meilleur*.**   [you can say **moins bon** or
> Your dish is better.   **aussi bon** but not '**plus bon**']

Meilleur will change to **meilleure**, **meilleurs**, **meilleures** according to the gender and number of the noun it is linked with.

You can also use **plus**, **moins** and **aussi** with *adverbs* exactly in the same way:

On se déplaçait *moins facilement.*
People moved around less easily.

Il travaille *plus rapidement* **qu'elle.**
He works more quickly than her.

Ce camion roule *aussi vite* **que nous.**
This lorry is going as fast as we are.

The only exception concerns **bien**:

On vivait *mieux.*	[you can say **moins bien** and
We lived better.	**aussi bien** but not '**plus bien**']
[life was better]	

Exercise 5

Translate the following sentences.

1 Life is harder.
2 We travel more easily.
3 I work as quickly.

4 My dessert is better.
5 I go on holiday less often.
6 It's better.

Language points

Comparing with plus, moins, autant

You can use **plus**, **moins**, **autant** with *verbs*:

Je *m'intéressais plus* **aux filles qu'à la guerre.**
I was more interested in girls than the war.

Il *travaille moins.*
He works less.

Il *mange* **toujours** *autant*?
Does he still eat as much/so much?

You can use **plus**, **moins**, **autant** followed by **de** with *nouns*:

On prenait *plus de temps* **pour faire les choses.**
We took more time to do things.

Evidemment, mes parents avaient *moins d'argent.*
Of course, my parents had less money.

Je n'avais jamais bu *autant de champagne*!
I had never drunk as much/so much champagne!

Je n'ai pas *autant de vêtements* que toi.
I haven't got as many clothes as you.

Exercise 6

Fill in the blanks with **plus**, **moins**, **autant** and **de** when appropriate.

1 Il a perdu 5 kilos. Il fait _____ sport et il mange _____ .
2 Il est beaucoup moins fatigué. Il travaille toujours _____ , mais il se repose un peu _____ .
3 J'ai perdu mon emploi. Alors tu comprends, j'ai _____ argent et _____ soucis [worries].
4 Elle est à la retraite depuis un an et elle est devenue très active. Elle cuisine _____ et elle passe _____ temps avec ses amis.

Exercise 7

Using the words below as prompts, compare what life was like in the 1950s to what it's like now.

Example: **Dans les années 50, on avait moins de vacances. Aujourd'hui, on a plus de temps.**

les vacances	le temps	l'argent
travailler	voyager	communiquer
le confort	stressé	heureux
la pollution	les guerres	

Language points

Using le plus, le moins

J'étais *le plus* jeune.
I was the younger/youngest.

C'était la voiture *la moins* chère.
It was the cheaper/cheapest car.

J'ai pris les tomates *les plus* mûres.
I took/bought the riper/ripest tomatoes.

As you can see from the examples above, the French do not make a distinction between the comparative form (the younger) and the superlative form (the youngest). But you will need to select the right article (**le**, **la**, **les**) according to the gender and number of the noun it is linked with.

Exercise 8

Look at these two hotel advertisements and answer the questions.

Hôtel du Parc	Hôtel Raymond
☆☆☆☆	☆☆☆
25 chambres	60 chambres
Chambre simple: 60 euros	Chambre simple: 50 euros
Chambre double: 80 euros	Chambre double: 60 euros
Télévision satellite, mini-bar dans toutes les chambres.	Télévision dans toutes les chambres.
Sauna, gym, piscine couverte, salon de coiffure 2 restaurants 3 cafés	Salon de coiffure 1 restaurant 1 café
30 minutes à pied du centre-ville	10 minutes à pied du centre-ville

Quel est l'hôtel ...

1 le moins cher?
2 le plus confortable?
3 avec le plus de chambres?
4 avec le moins de restaurants et de cafés?
5 le plus proche du centre-ville?

13 Rendez-vous et invitations

Appointments and invitations

> **In this unit you will learn about:**
> - using the simple future
> - using the conditional
> - expressing a condition with **si**
> - how to arrange a meeting and respond to an invitation

Dialogue 1 (Audio 2; 26)

Rendez-vous

Anne is going to Grenoble for business purposes and plans to pay her friend Marc Bressot a visit.

ANNE: Allô, est-ce que je pourrais parler à monsieur Bressot, s'il vous plaît?

EMPLOYEE: Oui, madame. Ne quittez pas.

ANNE: Allô Marc? C'est Anne à l'appareil.

MARC: Anne? Quel plaisir de vous entendre! Vous allez bien?

ANNE: Très bien, merci. Et vous?

MARC: Pareillement, merci.

ANNE: Marc, je serai à Grenoble la semaine prochaine et je me demandais... J'aimerais bien passer vous voir.

MARC: Ça me ferait énormément plaisir! Quand est-ce que vous pouvez venir?

ANNE: Je suis disponible mercredi matin et jeudi après-midi.

MARC: Alors, voyons. Je suis en réunion mercredi matin jusqu'à midi. Ah et malheureusement je suis en

	déplacement jeudi. Je vais voir des clients à Aix. Quel dommage!
ANNE:	Attendez! Je pourrais peut-être trouver un moment mercredi en fin d'après-midi. Je suis très occupée, mais je devrais être libre vers 4 heures. Ça vous conviendrait?
MARC:	C'est parfait.
ANNE:	Je téléphonerai à votre secrétaire mercredi vers 11 heures pour confirmer.

Vocabulary

ne quittez pas	hold the line	**l'appareil**	(*here*) the phone
pareillement	the same, similarly	**disponible**	free, available
une réunion	a meeting	**un déplacement**	a (business) trip
occupé	busy	**libre**	free
ça vous conviendrait?		would that be convenient for you?	

Language points

Talking about the future with the simple future

You already know how to talk about the future, using either the *present tense* or **aller** + *verb in the infinitive*.

> **Je *suis* en réunion *mercredi matin*.**
> I'm in a meeting Wednesday morning.

> **Nous *allons partir* en France *l'an prochain*.**
> We are going to go to France next year.

These two forms are by far the most frequently used when you want to talk about future events. However, there is also a tense called the simple future.

> **Je *serai* à Grenoble, la semaine prochaine.**
> I'll be in Grenoble next week.

> **Je *téléphonerai* à votre secrétaire mercredi vers 11 heures.**
> I will ring your secretary on Wednesday at 11 o'clock.

The simple future is normally confined to a certain number of situations. Try to use it when what you are saying contains a certain amount of:

- promise:

  Je *ferai* la vaisselle plus tard.
  I'll do the washing-up later.

  Je *téléphonerai* à votre secrétaire mercredi vers 11 heures.
  I'll ring your secretary on Wednesday at 11 o'clock.

- prediction, or is easily calculable from dates, diary etc.:

  Il *fera* beau sur l'ensemble de la France.
  It will be sunny everywhere in France.

  Ma fille *aura* 20 ans en 2010.
  My daughter will be 20 in 2010.

  Je *serai* à Grenoble, la semaine prochaine.
  I'll be in Grenoble next week.

How to form the simple future

With most verbs, the simple future uses for its stem the part of the infinitive that comes before the **-r**. For instance the stem for **aimer** will be **aime-** and for **vendre** it will be **vend-**. You simply then add the following endings: **-rai, -ras, -ra, -rons, -rez, -ront**:

j'aime*rai*	**nous aime*rons***
tu aime*ras*	**vous aime*rez***
il, elle, on aime*ra*	**ils, elles aime*ront***

The endings never change but some verbs have an irregular stem. Here are the most useful ones:

être	→	**se-**	→	**je serai**
avoir	→	**au-**	→	**j'aurai**
faire	→	**fe-**	→	**je ferai**
pouvoir	→	**pour-**	→	**je pourrai**
vouloir	→	**voud-**	→	**je voudrai**
devoir	→	**dev-**	→	**je devrai**
aller	→	**i-**	→	**j'irai**
venir	→	**viend-**	→	**je viendrai**

voir	→	ver-	→	je verrai
falloir	→	faud-	→	il faudra
savoir	→	sau-	→	je saurai

Exercise 1 🎧 (Audio 2; 27)

Put the verbs in brackets in the simple future.

1 Nous _____ (venir) l'année prochaine.
2 Il _____ (partir) tout seul.
3 Tu _____ (faire) la vaisselle?
4 Elles _____ (devoir) travailler dur.
5 J' _____ (avoir) 35 ans dans deux ans.
6 On _____ (pouvoir) sortir tous les soirs.
7 Vous _____ (prendre) du poisson?
8 Nous _____ (être) un peu en retard.

Exercise 2

You predict the future to a young friend of yours who is anxious to do well in his/her life. Play the part of the fortune-teller using the prompts below.

1 rencontrer l'homme/la femme de ta vie
2 avoir cinq enfants
3 gagner un million à la loterie
4 arrêter de travailler
5 acheter plusieurs maisons en France
6 vivre très longtemps

Language points

Using the conditional

This is a tense you have already come across several times during the course. It has a significant number of uses but is largely known as the tense of the unreal. This is because more often than not it will allow you to present something that might or might not happen.

With the verbs **vouloir**, **pouvoir** and **aimer** (**mieux**), it is often used to express a polite request, a wish, a preference or a suggestion:

Je *voudrais* une baguette, s'il vous plaît. (request)
I'd like a baguette, please.

Est-ce que je *pourrais* parler à monsieur Bressot, s'il vous plaît? (request)
Could I talk to Mr Bressot, please?

On *pourrait* aller à la piscine. (suggestion)
We could go to the swimming pool.

J'*aimerais* bien passer vous voir. (wish)
I'd like to come and see you.

J'*aimerais* mieux aller au cinéma. (preference)
I'd rather go to the cinema.

With **devoir**, it is often used to give advice or express a close certainty:

Tu *devrais* voir ton médecin. (advice)
You should see your doctor.

Je *devrais* être libre vers 4 heures. (close certainty)
I should/ought to be free around 4 o'clock.

How to form the conditional

Once you know how to form the simple future, it is very easy to form the conditional. The conditional uses exactly the same stem as the simple future. The endings for the conditional are: **-rais**, **-rais**, **-rait**, **-rions**, **-riez**, **-raient**.

Je *viendrais* bien avec vous.
I'd love to come with you.

Nous *serions* très heureux de vous recevoir.
We would be very happy to have you.

Ils *aimeraient* mieux travailler.
They'd rather work.

Exercise 3 (Audio 2; 29)

Respond to the following situations, using the conditional.

Example: **J'ai mal aux dents.** (give advice)
Tu devrais aller chez le dentiste.

1 Je suis fatigué.
   (give advice)

2 On va au cinéma?
   (express a preference to do something else)

3 Je m'ennuie.
   (make a suggestion)

4 J'ai envie de prendre un café. Et toi?
   (express your own wish)

5 Allô, agence de détectives Marlowe.
   (politely request to talk to a detective)

Language points

Talking about your availability

To talk about your availability, you can use the following structures:

Je *suis libre* demain matin.
I'm free tomorrow morning.

M. Martin *est disponible* toute la journée.
Mr. Martin is available all day.

Mme Deschamps *est occupée*.
Mrs Deschamps is busy.

You can also use:

Marc *est en réunion* toute la matinée.
Marc is in a meeting all morning.

Je *suis en déplacement* la semaine prochaine.
I'm on a business trip next week.

Pierre *est en congés*.
Pierre is on (annual) leave.

Nous *sommes en vacances* jusqu'au 20.
We are on holiday until the 20th.

Exercise 4

Juliette and Thomas are trying to meet. Here are their diaries.
Using the second half of Dialogue 1 as a model, try to recreate
their conversation.

JULIETTE	*lundi*	*mardi*
matin	réunion (9 h-11 h)	libre
après-midi	libre	réunion (2 h-5 h)
THOMAS	*lundi*	*mardi*
matin	libre	visite à des clients à Avignon
après-midi	réunion (2 h-5 h)	congés

THOMAS: Quand est-ce que vous pouvez venir?
JULIETTE: Je suis ...

Dialogue 2 🎧 (Audio 2; 30)

Une invitation

Anne is still in Grenoble visiting some clients. One of them, Philippe,
would like to invite her for a coffee.

PHILIPPE: Vous avez le temps de prendre un café?
ANNE: C'est gentil, Philippe. Je regrette, mais j'ai un rendez-
            vous dans un quart d'heure.
PHILIPPE: Peut-être plus tard, alors. Je serai libre vers 5 heures.
            On pourrait prendre un verre ensemble.
ANNE: Vous savez, je suis débordée aujourd'hui. Ça risque
            d'être difficile.
PHILIPPE: Demain alors?
ANNE: Euh, c'est à dire que j'ai des réunions toute la
            journée. Je ne vois pas quand j'aurai un moment.
PHILIPPE: Et si je vous invitais à dîner demain soir? Je connais
            un excellent restaurant italien qui fait des lasagnes
            fabuleuses! Vous aimez les lasagnes?

ANNE: J'adore, mais je ne sais pas à quelle heure je vais
            terminer. Et puis, j'ai ce rapport à préparer pour le
            lendemain. Ça va être très difficile.
PHILIPPE: Je vois.
ANNE: Je suis vraiment navrée. J'aimerais beaucoup sortir
            dîner avec vous, si j'avais le temps. Ecoutez, si je finis
            avant huit heures, je vous appellerai.

Vocabulary

prendre un verre	to have a drink	**débordé**	snowed under with work
un rapport	a report	**avoir le temps**	to have (the) time

Language points

Expressing a condition

To express a condition, you can use the following structures with **si**:

- when a possible event relies on something that has not yet happened:

si + present , simple future

Si je *finis* avant huit heures, je vous *appellerai*.
If I finish before 8, I will call you.

Tu *auras* un dessert, *si* tu *manges* tes légumes.
You'll have a dessert, if you eat your vegetables.

The tense in the main clause is often the *simple future* but you can also find the *imperative* as for example in Dialogue 2 of Unit 11, the *present* tense or **aller** + *verb in the infinitive*.

- when a hypothetical event relies on something that is not true/ real at the time:

si + imparfait , conditional

J'*aimerais* beaucoup sortir dîner avec vous, *si j'avais* le temps.
I would love to go out for a meal with you, if I had time.

Si tu *travaillais* plus, tu *aurais* de meilleurs résultats.
If you worked more, you would have better results.

In both cases **si** becomes **s'** when used with **il**:

S'il fait beau, nous irons à la plage.
If it's sunny, we'll go to the beach.

S'il faisait beau, nous irions à la plage.
If it were sunny, we would go to the beach.

Exercise 5 🎧 (Audio 2; 31)

A une condition! Some of your friends have made a few suggestions to you, but your answers depend on conditions. Make sentences, following the example.

Example: **Je viendrai avec vous à la campagne**
s'il ne pleut pas.

1 Un week-end à la plage   (pas de pluie)
2 Une sortie au cinéma   (ne pas finir trop tard au travail)
3 Une sortie au restaurant   (ne pas être fatigué)
4 Des vacances   (pouvoir prendre des congés)
5 Une journée à Paris   (être libre)

Exercise 6

Avec un peu d'imagination! Imagine what you would do if you won the Lottery. Make sentences following the example:

Example: **Si je gagnais à la loterie, je partirais en vacances.**

Language points

Did you notice?

When Philippe invited Anne for a meal, he used:

Et si je vous *invitais* à dîner demain soir?
What about dinner with me tomorrow night?

You can use this structure **si** + **imparfait** + **?** to make a suggestion or propose something.

> *Si* on *allait* **au cinéma?**
> What about going to the cinema?

Exercise 7

Respond to the following people by making a suggestion, using **si** with **imparfait**.

1 Il pleut. Qu'est-ce qu'on va faire?
2 Je travaille trop. Je suis stressé et déprimé.
3 J'ai pas envie de faire la cuisine ce soir.
4 Encore rien à la télévision!
5 Je me sens pas très bien.

Exercise 8

How much can you remember of the two dialogues in this unit? Fill in the blanks with the correct form of the verb in brackets, choosing between the simple future, present tense, conditional or **imparfait**.

1 Anne _____ (être) à Grenoble la semaine prochaine.
2 Elle _____ (vouloir) passer voir Marc.
3 Elle _____ (appeler) sa secrétaire pour confirmer le rendez-vous.
4 Anne _____ (aimer) dîner avec Philippe si elle _____ (avoir) le temps.
5 Elle _____ (appeler) Philippe si elle _____ (finir) avant huit heures.

14 Un week-end passé à cuisiner

A weekend spent cooking

In this unit you will learn about:

- using the imperative to give instructions
- using the pronouns **le**, **la**, **les**
- using the pronoun **en**
- expressions relating to cooking

Dialogue 1 🎧 (Audio 2; 32)

Une ratatouille réussie

Chantal and Jacques have invited a couple of friends, Daniel and Elise, for a barbecue. We join the two women as Chantal explains to Elise how to make ratatouille.

ELISE: Qu'est-ce que tu prépares de bon?

CHANTAL: Une ratatouille pour aller avec les côtes de porc et les merguez. Ça va, non?

ELISE: Mmm, j'adore la ratatouille, mais je ne sais vraiment pas la faire. C'est difficile?

CHANTAL: Non. Théoriquement tu dois faire cuire tous les légumes séparément mais moi, je ne le fais pas.

ELISE: Comment tu fais alors?

CHANTAL: Je fais d'abord revenir mes oignons dans de l'huile d'olive et puis j'ajoute les courgettes et les aubergines.

ELISE: Tu les mets au même moment?

CHANTAL: Oui et tu les fais cuire un peu à feu moyen. Et après, tu ajoutes les tomates.

ELISE: Tu les a épluchées?

CHANTAL: Oui, parce que Jacques n'aime pas la peau des tomates.

ELISE: Et c'est tout?

CHANTAL: Non, tu sales et tu poivres. Et tu mets du thym, du persil et une feuille de laurier. Voilà. Maintenant, on laisse mijoter 20 minutes. Bon, on a le temps de prendre un petit apéritif avec les hommes.

ELISE: On le prend sur la terrasse?

CHANTAL: Oui. Je sors les verres.

Vocabulary

une côte de porc	a pork chop
une merguez	a type of spicy sausage
faire cuire	to cook
faire revenir	(here) to brown
l'huile	oil
ajouter	to add
mettre	to put
à feu moyen	on a medium heat
éplucher	to peel
la peau	the skin
saler	to salt
poivrer	to pepper
le thym	thyme
le persil	parsley
une feuille	a leaf
le laurier	bay
faire/laisser mijoter	to simmer
un verre	a glass

Language points

Talking about cooking

The French love to talk about cooking. In Dialogue 1, Chantal uses the present tense to explain to Elise how to make a ratatouille. She uses the following verbs to talk about the recipe: **faire cuire**, **faire revenir**, **ajouter**, **mettre**, **éplucher**, **saler**, **poivrer**, **laisser mijoter**.

Here are a few more useful verbs you may need:

Vous *coupez* les tomates en quatre.
You cut the tomatoes in four.

Tu *mélanges* bien.
You mix well.

Tu *verses* la pâte dans un moule à gâteaux.
You pour the mixture into a cake tin.

Vous *faites griller* les steaks?
Are you grilling the steaks?

Elle *fait bouillir* l'eau pour les pâtes.
She's boiling the water for the pasta.

Exercise 1

When you look up a recipe in French cookery books, you will see that verbs tend to be in the infinitive. Here's the recipe for a vegetable flan. Explain the recipe to a friend, using the present tense.

Flan de légumes

3 courgettes
2 tomates bien grosses
2 œufs
1 litre de lait
sel
poivre
cumin
paprika

Préchauffer le four à 200 degrés. Couper les courgettes et les tomates en tranches d'un demi-centimètre. Dans un moule à flans, alterner une rangée de courgettes et une rangée de tomates. Mélanger les œufs au lait. Ajouter une pincée de sel, un peu de poivre, une cuillère à café de cumin et de paprika. Verser le mélange dans le moule. Mettre au four. Laisser cuire une heure.

Tu préchauffes le four à 200 degrés.

1 Tu _____

2 Ensuite _____

3 _____

4 _____

5 Et puis, _____

6 _____

7 _____

Language points

Using the pronouns le, la, les

Like all pronouns **le**, **la**, **les** are used to avoid repeating something which has already been mentioned. Like all pronouns, they are usually placed just before the verb they relate to. When used in the negative, the **ne** comes just before **le**, **la** or **les**.

le   usually replaces a masculine singular noun

la   replaces a feminine singular noun

les replaces a plural noun

Because they replace something which comes *directly* after the verb, something which is not preceded by a preposition such as **à** or **de** for example, they are called *direct object pronouns*.

Je prépare *l'apéritif.*	→	**Je** *le* **prépare.**
Je ne fais pas *la vaisselle.*	→	**Je ne** *la* **fais pas.**
Je regarde *les informations.*	→	**Je** *les* **regarde.**
but		
Je pense *à mes vacances.*	→	**J'y pense.**

In later units, you will come across indirect object pronouns; but in this unit, you will only work with verbs taking direct object pronouns. Here are a few examples from Dialogue 1:

Oui et tu <u>les</u> *fais cuire* **un peu à feu moyen.**
   (les aubergines et les courgettes)
Yes, and you cook *them* a little on a low heat.

Tu <u>les</u> *a épluchées?*   **(les tomates)**
Did you peel *them*?

J'adore la ratatouille, mais je ne sais pas vraiment la _faire_.
(la ratatouille)
I love ratatouille, but I don't really know how to make *it*.

On le _prend_ sur la terrasse?
(l'apéritif)
Are we having *it* on the terrace?

Le and **la** will drop the **-e** and **-a** in front of a verb starting with a vowel or an **h**.

Il restait une pomme, non? Wasn't there an apple left?
Je _l'_ai mangée, hier. I ate it yesterday.

Did you notice?

When you use **la** or **les** with a verb in the **passé composé**, the past participle agrees in gender and number with **la** (feminine singular) or **les** (masculine or feminine plural).

Tu _les_ a épluché*es*? (les tomates)
Non, je ne _les_ ai pas épluché*es*.

Où sont les verres à whisky?
Where are the whisky glasses?

Je _les_ ai rangé*s* dans le buffet.
I put them in the sideboard.

Et la nappe?
What about the tablecloth?

Je _l'_ai mis*e* dans le buffet aussi.
I put it in the sideboard, too.

Exercise 2

Read again the recipe in Exercise 1. What do the pronouns in italics replace?

1 On *le* préchauffe à 200 degrés.
2 On *les* coupe en tranches.
3 On *les* mélange au lait.
4 On *la* verse dans le moule.
5 On *le* met au four et on *le* laisse cuire une heure.

And in the following sentences, what do you think they replace?

6 On *le* prend tous les matins.
7 On *la* regarde tous les jours.
8 On *les* utilise pour ouvrir la porte.
9 On préfère *les* oublier.
10 On *l'*écrit et on *la* met dans une boîte.

Exercise 3 (Audio 2; 33)

In the following sentences fill in the gaps with **le**, **la**, **l'** or **les**.

1 Tu mets le sel quand? Je _____ mets maintenant.
2 Où est la nappe? Tu _____ trouveras dans le buffet.
3 Où est-ce que tu achètes tes fruits? Je _____ achète au marché.
4 Quand est-ce qu'ils ont construit leur maison? Ils _____ ont construite en 1970.
5 A quel moment est-ce que tu as mis les tomates? Je _____ ai mises en dernier.
6 Tu sais faire la ratatouille? Non je ne sais pas _____ faire.

Exercise 4

Now answer the questions following the example.

> *Example*: **Tu as pris les valises?**
> **Oui, je les ai prises.**

1 Tu as vu ce documentaire politique à la télévision hier soir?
   Oui, je _____ .
2 On fait cette partie de tennis, alors?
   Oui, on _____ .
3 Tu as trouvé tes clés?
   Oui, je _____ .
4 Tu n'as pas entendu la sonnette?
   Non, je _____ .
5 Vous avez pris votre parapluie?
   Oui, je _____ .
6 Vous taperez ce rapport pour demain?
   Oui, je _____ .
7 Tu as mis mes lettres à la boîte?
   Non, je _____ . J'ai oublié!

Dialogue 2 🎧 (Audio 2; 34)

Comment allumer un barbecue

Jacques and Daniel are preparing the barbecue.

DANIEL: Il est super, ton barbecue! Tu l'as construit toi-même?

JACQUES: Oui, avec un copain bricoleur. J'en avais marre de ces barbecues que tu trouves dans le commerce et qui ne marchent jamais.

DANIEL: Comment tu l'allumes? Moi, je suis nul pour ce genre de choses.

JACQUES: Ben, c'est facile. Tiens, tu vas le faire. Prends ce papier journal, là sur la table. Froisse-le un peu et pose-le sur les cendres. Voilà.

DANIEL: Je ne les enlève pas avant?

JACQUES: Non, laisse-les. Ce n'est pas la peine.

DANIEL: J'allume?

JACQUES: Non, attends. Il faut mettre le charbon de bois. Alors, ne le mets pas tout d'un coup. Tu en verses juste un peu. Voilà, parfait. Maintenant, tu peux allumer. Bien.

DANIEL: Ça marche bien, on dirait. J'en mets un peu plus?

JACQUES:	Oui, vas-y. Ajoute un peu plus de charbon maintenant. Parfait.
DANIEL:	Et maintenant?
JACQUES:	Et maintenant, on attend un peu. Quand il n'y aura plus de flammes, tu pourras mettre les merguez et les côtes de porc. En attendant, si on prenait un petit apéro?
DANIEL:	Ah, ça oui. J'en ai bien besoin. Tu as du whisky?
JACQUES:	J'en ai acheté juste pour toi! Allons-y!

Vocabulary

toi-même	yourself	**un copain** (*fam.*)	friend, mate
un bricoleur	DIY man	**en avoir marre**	to be fed up
marcher	(*here*) to work, function	**jamais**	never
allumer	to light	**le charbon de bois**	charcoal
nul	(*fam.*) useless, hopeless	**froisser**	to crumple
poser	to put, to lay	**la cendre**	ash
enlever	to remove	**laisser**	to leave, to let
tout d'un coup	all at once	**en attendant**	while we are waiting

Language points

Using en

En is another pronoun which allows you to avoid repeating some information. **En** normally replaces a noun preceded by **de**, **du**, **de la**, **des**. Like **y**, **le**, **la**, **les**, it is normally placed directly before the verb.

> **Vous avez *des tomates*?**
> **Oui, j'*en* ai.**

> **J'*en* ai acheté juste pour toi. (du whisky)**
> I bought some just for you.

En can also be used when the noun it replaces is preceded by expressions of quantity such as **un**, **une**, **deux**, **trois**, etc., **un peu**

de, beaucoup de, assez de, un verre de, un kilo de, plusieurs, quelques, une dizaine, etc. In cases like this, the expression of quantity will follow the verb.

Vous avez une voiture?
Oui, j'*en* ai *une*.

Vous voulez *de la tarte*?
Oui, j'*en* veux *un peu*, s'il vous plaît. (un peu de tarte)

Tu *en* verses *juste un peu*. (un peu de charbon de bois)
You just put some of it.

Il prend *du vin* aux repas?
Oui, il *en* prend *un verre* à tous les repas. (un verre de vin)

Vous voulez *des pommes*?
Oui, j'*en* prendrai *une dizaine*, s'il vous plaît.
(une dizaine de pommes)
Yes, I'll have about ten, please.

Approximate numbers

une dizaine	une quinzaine
une vingtaine	une trentaine
une quarantaine	une cinquantaine
une soixantaine	une centaine
une douzaine = exactly 12	

En is also frequently used with some expressions such as:

J'*en* ai marre! (du travail, de la pluie, des enfants)
I'm fed up! (with work, rain, the children)

J'*en* ai bien besoin! (in Dialogue 2, **d'un apéritif**)
I really need it!

Exercise 5 🎧 (Audio 2; 35)

Answer the questions, following the example.

Example: **Vous avez du pain?**
          Oui, j'en ai.

1 Vous prenez du riz?
   Oui, _____ .
2 Tu achèteras des tomates?
   Oui, _____ .
3 Vous voulez de la tarte au citron?
   Non, _____ .
4 Vous mangez souvent des légumes?
   Non, _____ .
5 Vous avez acheté du pain pour ce soir?
   Oui, nous _____ .

Exercise 6

On n'en a jamais assez! Imagine you are a multi-millionaire answering the following questions. Use **en** and expressions of quantity as in the example.

>   *Example*: **Vous avez combien de paires de chaussures?**
>   **J'en ai une cinquantaine.** *Or*: **J'en ai beaucoup.**

1 Vous avez combien de voitures?
2 Vous avez une maison secondaire?
3 Vous avez une piscine?
4 Vous avez des soucis?
5 Vous avez des œuvres d'art?

Language points

Giving instructions with the imperative

You have already encountered the imperative in Unit 11. The imperative is used to give instructions. There are three forms:

Prends **ce papier journal.**   (**tu** form)
Take this newspaper.

Venez **avec nous.**   (**vous** form)
Come with us.

Partons **à la plage.**   (**nous** form)
Let's go to the beach.

If you need to use a pronoun such as **le**, **la**, **les**, **en** or **y**, remember that it will be placed straight after the verb, unless the sentence is in the negative.

Froisse-*le* un peu et pose-*le* sur les cendres.
Crumple it a little and put it on the ashes.

Laisse-*les*.   **Vas-*y*.**
Leave them.   Go on.

Prenez-*en* un morceau.
Take a piece.

<u>Ne</u> *le* mets <u>pas</u> tout d'un coup.
Don't put it all at once.

As explained in Unit 11, most verbs use the present tense to form the imperative. But there are exceptions. Here are two: **être** and **avoir**.

Sois **gentil!**   (**tu** form)
Be good!

Soyez **prêts à huit heures.**   (**vous** form)
Be ready at eight.

Aie **de la patience.**   (**tu** form)
Be patient.

Ayez **du courage!**   (**vous** form)
Be brave!

Exercise 7 🎧 (Audio 2; 36)

Transform the following sentences, putting the verbs in the imperative as in the example.

Example: **La serviette? Tu la mets dans l'assiette.**
            Mets-la dans l'assiette.

1 Le vase? Tu le mets sur la table.
2 Nous prenons un taxi.
3 Du persil? Vous en achetez un peu.
4 Les cendres? Tu les laisses dans le barbecue.
5 Nous y allons tout de suite.
6 La ratatouille? Tu la fais pour demain.
7 Tu seras gentil avec elle.
8 Tu ne la laisseras pas toute seule.

Exercise 8

Do Exercise 1 again, but this time, use the imperative.

Préchauffe le four à 200 degrés.

1 _____ .
2 Ensuite _____ .
3 _____ .
4 _____ .
5 Et puis, _____ .
6 _____ .
7 _____ .

15 Vêtements et chaussures

Clothes and shoes

In this unit you will learn about:

* using **lequel, lesquels, laquelle, lesquelles**
* using **celui-ci, celui-là**, etc.
* using **ne . . . que**
* using expressions such as **ça me plaît**
* talking about colour, material and size
* using **quelque chose, quelqu'un**

Dialogue 1 🎧 (Audio 2; 37)

Le noir me va bien

Jacques has to exchange a shirt his wife bought him as a present.

JACQUES: Oui, bonjour. Je voudrais changer cette chemise, s'il vous plaît. La taille est bonne mais je n'aime pas beaucoup les rayures. Je préférerais de l'uni.

VENDEUR: Voyons la taille. C'est du L. Alors en L, je vais avoir ce modèle en rose pâle, blanc ou bleu ciel. J'aurais peut-être votre taille dans un autre modèle. Oui, en noir et en bordeaux.

JACQUES: La rose pâle, elle est en coton?

VENDEUR: 50% coton, 50% lin, monsieur.

JACQUES: Mmm, ça se froisse beaucoup, le lin.

VENDEUR: J'ai aussi ce modèle en 70% coton et 30% acrylique. Elle plaît beaucoup parce qu'on n'a pas besoin de la repasser.

JACQUES: Oui, mais je n'aime pas ce vert. Et puis, avec l'acrylique on transpire beaucoup. Je préférerais 100% coton.

VENDEUR: Alors, ce sera la noire ou la bordeaux. Elles sont en solde, d'ailleurs.

JACQUES: Bon, ben je vais prendre la noire. Le noir me va bien. Et puis, j'ai remarqué le beau pull en vitrine. Vous avez ma taille?

Vocabulary

une chemise	a shirt	**l'uni**	plain (colour)
la taille	the size	**les rayures**	stripes
en L	in Large	**rose pâle**	pale pink
bleu ciel	sky blue	**blanc**	white
noir	black	**bordeaux**	burgundy
le lin	linen	**elle plaît beaucoup**	it is very popular
repasser	to iron	**vert**	green
transpirer	to sweat	**en solde**	reduced (sale price)
en vitrine	in the window	**un pull**	a jumper
100% (cent pour cent)	one hundred per cent		

Language points (Audio 2; 38)

Talking about colours, material and size

To talk about colours, materials and sizes, you can use the following structure:

> **en** + colour / material / size

Je voudrais cette chemise *en blanc*.
I'd like this shirt in white.

Je vais avoir ce modèle *en rose pâle, blanc ou bleu ciel*.
I'll have this style in pale pink, white or sky blue.

La rose pâle, elle est *en coton*?
The pale pink (shirt), is it cotton?

J'ai aussi ce modèle *en 70% coton et 30% acrylique*.
I also have this style in 70% cotton and 30% acrylic.

Nous avons ce pull *en S*.
We have this jumper in Small.

Alors *en L*, je vais avoir ce modèle.
So in Large, I have this style.

Colours can be *nouns* as in the above construction or *adjectives*. Unless you are using the above construction with **en** or are talking about the colour in general, and in that case the noun will be masculine singular, both adjectives and nouns will vary in gender and number with what they refer to.

Je voudrais une chemise *blanche*. (adjective)
I'd like a white shirt.

J'aime beaucoup cette fleur *rose*. Qu'est-ce que c'est? (adjective)
I like this pink flower very much. What is it?

J'adore *le noir*! (noun: the colour)
I love black.

Alors, ce sera *la noire* ou *la bordeaux*.
(nouns: the shirts defined by their colour)
So, it will be the black (one) or the burgundy (one).

Note that there are some exceptions. When a colour is derived from a fruit, a stone, a plant, a substance, a wine such as **bordeaux** for instance, the colour will not vary in gender and number.

J'adore ces roses *orange*.
I love these orange roses.

Cultural point

Though the French have their own numbering system for sizes, most clothes and shoes labels now include the equivalent size for the UK, Germany, Italy and the US. As in most countries, sizes for clothes tend to be reduced to S for small, M for medium, L for large and XL for extra large. Half sizes for shoes are not uncommon, so it is worth asking.

Les matières

le cuir	leather	la laine	wool
le coton	cotton	la soie	silk
le lin	linen	le nylon	nylon
l'acrylique	acrylic	le velours	velvet

Exercise 1

Read the following sentences and try to guess the meaning of the colours underlined.

1 <u>Jaune</u> comme un citron ou le soleil.
2 <u>Rouge</u> comme une tomate.
3 <u>Vert</u> comme les épinards.
4 <u>Marron</u> comme le chocolat au lait.
5 <u>Violet</u> comme une violette.

Now match the following
items of clothing
(p. 184) to
the right
drawing.

1	une veste	7	un pantalon
2	des chaussettes	8	une robe
3	une jupe à rayures	9	des sous-vêtements
4	un manteau	10	un blouson en cuir
5	un maillot de bains	11	un short
6	un jean	12	des gants

Exercise 2

Using the vocabulary provided and **en**, complete the sentences below.

1 Je n'aime pas beaucoup la couleur de cette jupe. Vous l'avez _____?

2 Il porte souvent un vieux pantalon _____ .

velours   vert

3 Marie adore les sous-vêtements _____ .

4 Je voudrais voir ces gants marron. Ils sont _____?

cuir   soie

5 Cette chemise noire elle est _____?

6 J'aime beaucoup ce maillot de bains dans la vitrine. Vous l'auriez _____?

coton   jaune

Exercise 3 🎧 (Audio 2; 39)

Can you say the following things in French?

1 I love red.
2 I would like black socks.
3 I like these gloves. Do you have them in brown?
4 He bought a leather jacket.
5 Do you have this skirt in Small?
6 I like this blue shirt but I prefer the pink one.

Language points

Did you notice?

When talking about size, you can use or will hear the following:

Vous avez ma taille?
Do you have my size?

Vous faites quelle taille?
What is your size?

Je fais du S.
I am size Small.

Vous chaussez du combien?
or **Vous faites quelle pointure?**
What size of shoes do you take?

Je fais du 38.
I take size 38.

Dialogue 2 ♀ (Audio 2; 40)

Celles-ci ou celles-là?

Chantal is shopping for shoes. When we join her in the shop, the shopkeeper is on the phone.

VENDEUSE: Je vais devoir raccrocher. J'ai quelqu'un dans le magasin. Je peux vous aider, madame?
CHANTAL: Oui, j'ai vu des chaussures blanches dans la vitrine. J'aimerais les essayer, s'il vous plaît.
VENDEUSE: Mais bien sûr, madame. Vous pouvez me les montrer? Lesquelles? Celles-ci?
CHANTAL: Non, celles-là avec le petit talon.
VENDEUSE: Vous faites quelle pointure?
CHANTAL: Du 37.
VENDEUSE: Je suis désolée. Je n'ai plus votre pointure dans cette couleur. Il ne reste que du noir.
CHANTAL: Non, je voudrais des chaussures blanches ou crème.
VENDEUSE: Je peux vous proposer celles-ci avec un tout petit peu plus de talon. On vient de les recevoir. Ou bien celles-là qui sont très bien aussi. On les a en blanc et en crème.
CHANTAL: Non, elles ne me plaisent pas beaucoup. Je préférerais quelque chose de plus habillé. Et celles-là, là? Vous ne les avez qu'en bleu marine?
VENDEUSE: Oui, je regrette.
CHANTAL: C'est vraiment dommage. Elles sont très belles et pas chères. J'ai quand même envie de les essayer, si vous avez ma pointure.

VENDEUSE: Malheureusement pas. C'est la dernière paire et c'est du 39.

CHANTAL: Décidément! Ce n'est pas mon jour de chance! Je ne vais rien trouver.

Vocabulary

raccrocher	to hang up	**le magasin**	the shop
aider	to help	**des chaussures** (f.)	shoes
la vitrine	the shop window	**essayer**	to try
montrer	to show	**rester**	(here) to be left
un talon	a heel	**bleu marine**	navy blue
habillé	formal (when talking about clothes or shoes)		

Language points

Using lequel, lesquels . . . celui-ci, celui-là . . .

Lequel, **laquelle**, **lesquels**, **lesquelles** are used to ask the question 'which one(s)'.

Since they stand for a noun, they change their form according to the gender (masculine or feminine) and the number (singular or plural) of the noun(s) they refer to.

Celui-ci, **celui-là**, **celle-ci**, **celle-là**, **ceux-ci**, **ceux-là**, **celles-ci**, **celles-là** are often used to answer the question starting with **lequel**, **laquelle**, etc. and can be translated by 'this/that one', 'these/those ones'. Like **lequel**, **laquelle** . . . they change their form according to the gender and number of the noun(s) they refer to.

Singular		Plural	
Masculine	*Feminine*	*Masculine*	*Feminine*
Lequel?	**Laquelle**?	**Lesquels**?	**Lesquelles**?
Which one?	Which one?	Which ones?	Which ones?
celui-ci/ **celui-là**	**celle-ci**/ **celle-là**	**ceux-ci**/ **ceux-là**	**celles-ci**/ **celles-là**
this one/ that one	this one/ that one	these ones/ those ones	these ones/ those ones

The French are not very particular about the difference between *this* and *that*, *these* and *those*. They will often prefer to use **celui-là** or **celle-là**, **ceux-là** or **celles-là** when in English you would use *this one* or *these ones*.

J'aime bien *ce chapeau*.
I like this hat.

***Lequel*?**
Which one?

***Cette jupe* me plaît bien.**
I like this skirt.

Moi, je préfère *celle-là*.
I prefer that one.

J'ai vu *des chaussures* dans la vitrine.
I've seen some shoes in the window.

***Lesquelles*?**
Which ones?

Celles-là.
These.

Tu as vu *ces gants* rouges! Ils sont vraiment sympa.
Have you seen these red gloves? They are really nice.

J'aime mieux *ceux-là*.
I prefer those.

Exercise 4

Fill in the gaps with the correct form of **lequel** and **celui-ci, celui-là**, etc.

1 – Regarde cette chemise bleue! Elle me plaît beaucoup.

   – Moi, je préfère _____ .

2 – J'ai vu un pull dans la vitrine.
   – Montrez-moi. C'est _____ ?

3 – Alors dans votre taille, je vais avoir ce modèle en vert ou
       _____ avec des rayures.
   – J'ai horreur des rayures.

4 – J'aime bien ces chaussures blanches. Il y a aussi ces noires
avec un peu de talon.
– _____ est-ce que tu préfères toi?

5 – Je cherche des gants en cuir noir.
– Nous avons _____ .

Language points

Using ne . . . que

Ne . . . que is usually translated as *only*. You can use **ne . . . que**
in the same way as **ne . . . pas**, **ne . . . plus** or **ne . . . jamais**. **Ne** is
always placed before the verb and **que** just before the word(s) it
directly refers to. These are underlined in the examples below.

> **Il *n*'aime *que* <u>les films d'horreur</u>.**
> He only likes horror films.

> **Nous *ne* prenons des vacances *qu*'<u>en été</u>.**
> We take holidays only in the summer.

> **Il *ne* reste *que* <u>du noir</u>.**
> There's only black left.

> **Vous *ne* les avez *qu*'<u>en bleu marine</u>?**
> Do you only have them in navy blue?

Exercise 5

Corinne est une femme avec des goûts de luxe. Using **ne . . . que**
and the words in brackets, make sentences, following the example.
Use your imagination for the last two examples.

> *Example*: **Les vacances _____ (faire des croisières)**
> **Ses vacances? Elle ne fait que des croisières.**

1 Les vêtements _____ .
(acheter des marques de grands couturiers)

2 La musique _____ .
(aller à des concerts de grands musiciens)

3 Le dimanche midi _____ .
(manger du caviar et boire du champagne)

4 Les voitures _____ .
   (acheter des modèles de luxe)

5 Les amis _____ .

6 Le sport _____ .

Gabriel est un homme difficile. Using **ne ... que**, imagine what he is like and make sentences following the model above.

7 Le cinéma   Il n'aime que _____ .
8 Les vêtements
9 La nourriture
10 La musique

Language points

Did you notice?

J'ai *quelqu'un* dans le magasin.
I have someone in the shop.

Je préférerais *quelque chose* de plus habillé.
I'd prefer something more formal.

Though **quelqu'un** means 'someone' and **quelque chose** means 'something', **quelqu'un** can also be translated by 'anyone' and **quelque chose** by 'anything'.

Il y a *quelqu'un*?
Is there someone/anyone there?

Je ne cherche pas *quelque chose* de particulier.
I'm not looking for something/anything in particular.

Ne ... personne means 'no one' and **ne ... rien** means 'nothing'. But here again, **ne ... personne** can be translated by 'not ... anyone' and **ne ... rien** by 'not ... anything'.

Il *n'*y a *personne* ici.
There's no one here/ There isn't anyone here.

Je *ne* vais *rien* faire.
I am not going to do anything/ I am going to do nothing.

Ne ... personne and **ne ... rien** can be paired with another negative form such as **ne ... jamais** or **ne ... plus**.

> **Il *ne* voit *plus personne*.**
> He no longer sees anyone./He doesn't see anybody any more.

> **Je *ne* trouve *jamais rien* dans ce magasin.**
> I never find anything in this shop.

Exercise 6

Pair the following captions with the drawings.

1 Il y a quelqu'un?
2 Il ne gagne jamais rien, mais il continue à jouer.
3 Vous n'avez pas quelque chose de plus cool?
4 Elle fait sa crise d'adolescence. Elle ne veut parler à personne.

Exercise 7

Translate the following.

1 I don't want anything, thank you.
2 He likes no one.
3 Are you looking for something?
4 I saw someone.
5 They never find anything in this shop.

Exercise 8

Read the text and answer the questions in English.

SI ON ALLAIT À LA BROCANTE

Les Français sortent de plus en plus fréquemment. Ils se promènent, voyagent, vont à des expositions ou visitent des musées, acceptent des invitations à dîner, fréquentent les boîtes de nuit et les bars de plus en plus nombreux, vont manger au restaurant . . .

Mais ces dernières années, les Français ont découvert une nouvelle forme de loisirs: la brocante. Cette activité relativement récente s'est répandue dans beaucoup de villes et de villages. Le plaisir consiste à chercher et parfois trouver l'objet rare, le vieux sofa du début du siècle dernier ou la première édition d'un *Tintin*. Trouvera? Trouvera pas? Et à quel prix? Les prix pratiqués varient beaucoup et il faut s'y connaître un peu pour éviter les mauvaises surprises. Une belle peinture montrant un cheval de labours accroche mon regard. "Ça date du 18e siècle", me dit le vendeur. Le prix? 120 euros tout juste. En réalité, c'est un faux, vendu dans un modeste magasin de décoration pour un modeste prix de 30 euros. Comment est-ce que je le sais, me direz-vous? Euh, le magasin m'appartient.

Vocabulary

découvrir	to discover	**varier**	to vary
s'y connaître	to have a good knowledge	**éviter**	to avoid
mauvais	bad	**accrocher**	(*here*) to hold
regard	(*here*) eye	**cheval de labours**	plough-horse

1 List the activities mentioned in the first paragraph.
2 What do you think is a **brocante**?
3 What do you think **s'est répandue** means?
4 Is the painting that caught the journalist's eye genuine?
5 How does he know?

16 On cherche une maison

Looking for a house

In this unit you will learn about:

- using the relative pronouns **qui**, **que**, **où**
- expressing your opinion
- talking about the future with **quand**
- using **il y a** and **dans**
- using prepositions to express position
- using **trop (de)** and **assez (de)**

Dialogue 1 (Audio 2; 42)

On cherche

Jacques and Chantal are looking for a smaller house to buy. They have done some preliminary research and are talking about it.

JACQUES: Regarde celle-là. Maison de caractère rénovée, cuisine meublée, séjour, trois chambres, beau panorama.

CHANTAL: Tu ne trouves pas que c'est un peu grand? A mon avis, on n'a pas besoin de trois chambres. Deux, ça suffit largement. Tu sais, Christine a presque terminé ses études et quand elle aura un travail, elle viendra moins souvent à la maison.

JACQUES: Mmm, tu as raison, mais j'aimerais bien avoir un peu de terrain quand même. Je voudrais aussi une pièce pour bricoler. Quand je serai à la retraite, j'ai bien l'intention de rester occupé.

CHANTAL: Oui, moi aussi. Il me faut un jardin de toute façon. Je ne m'imagine pas sans plantes! Et ça, qu'est-ce que c'est?

JACQUES: C'est une annonce que j'ai trouvée sur internet.
CHANTAL: Voyons. Jolie maison neuve qui offre une surface habitable de 120 m², deux chambres, grande cuisine, jardin, terrasse...
JACQUES: Elle est où?
CHANTAL: Alors, elle est à cinq minutes d'un petit village où on trouve toutes les commodités. Mais ils ne disent pas lequel.
JACQUES: J'en ai une autre, là. Attends. Mmm, je crois qu'elle est un peu chère pour notre budget. 250 000 euros.
CHANTAL: Oh oui, dis-donc. C'est pas dans nos prix. Je pense qu'on devrait téléphoner à Mme Duclos.
JACQUES: Mme Duclos?
CHANTAL: C'est la dame qui dirige la nouvelle agence immobilière. Elle a l'air très sympathique.

Vocabulary

une maison de caractère		a house with character	
une cuisine meublée		a fitted/furnished kitchen	
un séjour	a living room	**une chambre**	a bedroom
penser	to think	**ça suffit**	that's enough
un terrain	a plot	**avoir du terrain**	to have land (around a house)
une pièce	a room	**bricoler**	to do DIY
une plante	a plant	**une annonce**	an advertisement
une surface habitable	a surface area	**les commodités**	amenities
croire	to believe, to think	**diriger**	to be in charge of
une agence immobilière		an estate agency	
m² (mètre carré)		square metre	

Language points

Using the relative pronouns qui, que *and* où

The relative pronouns **qui** and **que** relate either to persons or to things in order to provide additional information about the person(s) or thing(s), much like an adjective would. Both **qui** and **que** can be translated by 'who(m)', 'which', 'that' or nothing!

In French the use of **qui** and **que** depends on the grammatical relation between the word(s) coming before them and the verb that follows them. Unlike their English equivalents, **qui** and **que** cannot be omitted in French.

Because **qui** is the *subject* of the verb that follows it, you cannot use, for example, **je**, **tu**, **il**, **elle**, etc., after it.

Jolie maison neuve *qui* offre une surface habitable de 120 m².
Attractive new house that/which offers a surface area of 120 m².

C'est la dame *qui* dirige la nouvelle agence immobilière.
It's the woman who runs the new estate agency.

Because **que** is the *object* of the verb that follows it, it is always followed by a subject (for example **je**, **tu**, **il**, **elle**, etc.) and its verb.

C'est une annonce *que* j'ai trouvée sur internet.
It is an advert (that/which) I found on the internet.

Je vais te présenter à quelqu'un *que* tu ne connais pas.
I am going to introduce you to someone (that/whom) you don't know.

Note that, when used with a verb in the **passé composé**, the past participle of the verb following **que** will agree in gender and number with the noun(s) it relates to. The noun(s) are underlined in the examples below.

C'est <u>une femme</u> *que* j'ai connu*e* à Paris.
<u>Les fruits</u> *que* tu as acheté*s* sont très bons.

The relative pronoun **où** usually relates to a place and can be translated as 'where'.

Elle est à cinq minutes d'un petit village *où* on trouve toutes les commodités.
It's five minutes from a little village where you can find all amenities.

C'est le bureau *où* je travaille.
It's the office where I work.

Exercise 1 🎧 (Audio 2; 43)

Fill in the gaps with *qui*, *que* or *où*.

- Vous connaissez Mme Duclos?
- Oui, c'est une femme (1) _____ j'aime beaucoup. C'est elle (2) _____ dirige la nouvelle agence immobilière.
- Une nouvelle agence immobilière? Où ça?
- A côté de la poste, dans un ancien magasin de vêtements de sport (3) _____ a fermé, l'an dernier.
- Le magasin (4) _____ la femme du maire travaillait?
- Oui, c'est ça. D'ailleurs, c'est elle (5) _____ a écrit un petit article sur Mme Duclos.
- Ah bon?
- Oui, c'est un article (6) _____ j'ai trouvé très amusant. Apparemment, Mme Duclos connaissait bien le maire quand elle était jeune. Il envoyait souvent des fleurs à l'agence (7) _____ elle travaillait.

Exercise 2

Combine the two sentences, using **qui**, **que** or **où**.

> *Example*: **Versailles est un château. Il se trouve dans la région parisienne**
> **Versailles est un château qui se trouve dans la région parisienne.**

1 Les oranges sont des fruits d'hiver. Elles sont riches en vitamine C.
2 *La Chute* est un roman de Camus. Je l'aime beaucoup.
3 La Loire est une région magnifique. On y trouve d'excellents vins blancs doux.
4 François Mitterrand était un homme politique contesté. Il avait ses partisans.
5 C'est Patrick. Je l'ai rencontré en vacances en Italie.

Language points

Expressing your opinion

You can express your opinion using the following structures:

> *Tu ne trouves pas que* **c'est un peu grand?**
> Don't you think (that) it's a little big?

*Je pense qu'***on devrait téléphoner à Mme Duclos.**
I think (that) we should/ought to ring Mme Duclos.

*Je crois qu'***elle est un peu chère pour notre budget.**
I think (that) it's a little too expensive for our budget.

Unlike its English equivalent 'that', **que** cannot be omitted in French.

A mon avis, **on n'a pas besoin de trois chambres.**
In my opinion, we don't need three bedrooms.

Tu as raison.   *Tu as tort.*
You are right.   You are wrong.

Exercise 3

Using some of the expressions you have just learned, give your views on the following.

> *Example*: **l'énergie solaire**
>   **Je trouve que c'est bien.**

1 les téléphones portables
2 les supermarchés
3 les transports publics
4 le recyclage (recycling)
5 l'écologie

Language points

Did you notice?

Quand **elle** *aura* **un travail, elle viendra moins souvent à la maison.**
When she has a job, she will come home less often.

Quand **je** *serai* **à la retraite, j'ai bien l'intention de rester occupé.**
When I retire, I intend to keep busy.

When you want to talk about future events with **quand**, the verb that follows **quand** will normally be in the future tense.

Exercise 4

Finish the following sentences, using the vocabulary in the box.

1 Il a l'intention d'acheter une nouvelle maison quand _____ .

2 Nadine veut visiter le musée du Louvre quand _____ .

3 Quand nous _____ , j'aimerais planter un ou deux palmiers.

4 Quand Paul et Thierry _____ , ils veulent devenir pilotes d'avion.

5 Je ne sais pas quand je _____ .

être à Paris être grand pouvoir téléphoner

être à la retraite refaire le jardin

Dialogue 2 (Audio 2; 44)

On visite

Jacques and Chantal are visiting a house they found through Mme Duclos. They are greeted by the owner of the house, Laure Breton, a retired woman.

CHANTAL: Vous avez une bien belle maison, madame. Et quelle vue magnifique!

LAURE: Oui, elle va bien me manquer. J'ai hésité longtemps et puis finalement j'ai décidé de vendre. Je ne suis plus très jeune, vous savez. Il y a six mois, je me suis cassé la jambe et depuis, j'ai du mal à marcher. Et puis, ce grand jardin, c'est trop de travail pour une femme seule. Mon mari est mort il y a deux ans. C'est lui qui s'occupait de tout. Mais, suivez-moi. Voilà la cuisine. Tout marche. Il y a une petite fuite à l'évier, mais le plombier passe dans quelques jours pour réparer.

JACQUES: Il y a une buanderie?

LAURE: Oui, juste derrière la cuisine. J'y range toutes mes provisions et il y a assez de place pour installer un séchoir et une planche à repasser.

CHANTAL: Ah, oui, en effet. C'est bien pratique.
LAURE: Voilà le salon, la salle à manger avec vue sur le jardin.
CHANTAL: C'est très lumineux. J'aime beaucoup la décoration. Et vous avez des objets magnifiques. J'adore ce vase sur le buffet. Il est très original!
LAURE: C'est mon mari qui l'a ramené d'Egypte. Et la peinture sur soie au-dessus de la cheminée vient du Congo. Mon mari et moi, nous avons beaucoup voyagé.
JACQUES: Je n'ai pas vu de garage.
LAURE: Non, il n'y en a pas. Mais mon mari a construit un atelier attenant à la buanderie. Il y réparait des horloges et des montres. C'était son passe-temps favori. Il y aussi une cave sous la buanderie. Elle est assez grande pour y stocker du vin.

Vocabulary

elle va me manquer	I'm going to miss it	**avoir du mal à**	to find it difficult to
tout	everything	**marcher**	(*here*) to work, function
une fuite	leak	**un évier**	sink

le plombier	plumber	**une buanderie**	utility room
ranger	to tidy up	**des provisions**	food (supplies)
un séchoir	clothes-horse	**une planche à repasser**	ironing board
ramener	to bring back	**une peinture**	painting
la cheminée	fireplace	**construire**	to build
un atelier	workshop	**attenant**	adjoining
une horloge	clock	**une montre**	watch
un passe-temps	a hobby		

Language points

Using il y a *and* dans

Il y a + *period of time* can be used to locate a past event, and is normally translated by *period of time* + 'ago'.

Il y a six mois, je me suis cassé la jambe.
Six months ago, I broke my leg.

Mon mari est mort il y a deux ans.
My husband died two years ago.

Dans + *period of time* can be used to locate a future event, and can be translated by 'in' + *period of time*.

Le plombier passe *dans quelques jours* pour réparer.
The plumber is coming in a few days to repair it.

Je pars en vacances *dans un mois*.
I'm going on holiday in a month.

Exercise 5

Fill in the gaps with **dans** or **il y a**.

1 Je suis prêt _____ cinq minutes.
2 Il est parti _____ une heure.
3 _____ vingt mille ans, l'homme n'existait pas.
4 Elle passe ses examens _____ quinze jours.
5 _____ combien de temps est-ce que tu seras prête?
6 Il a passé son permis de conduire _____ cinquante ans.

Language points

Some prepositions to talk about the position of things

Le chat est *sur* le lit.
Les chaussures sont *sous* le lit.

Le piano est *derrière* le lit.
Le tabouret est *devant* le piano.

Le tapis est *au-dessous du* lit.
Le poster est *au-dessus du* lit.

Remember that the **de** in **au-dessus de** and **au-dessous de** will combine with the articles **le** and **les** to give respectively **du** and **des**.

Exercise 6

Using your own house or a fictitious one, imagine where the following items would be located. Use as many as you can of the prepositions that you've just learned.

Example: **Il y a une salle de bains au-dessus de la cuisine.**

1 une antenne (an aerial)
2 un jardin
3 une terrasse
4 une cour
5 une cave
6 un grenier (an attic)
7 une buanderie

Language points

Using trop (de) **and** assez (de)

You can use **assez** and **trop** in front of adjectives and adverbs.
Assez is usually translated by 'enough', 'rather' or 'quite' depending
on the context, and **trop** by 'too'.

Elle est *assez* **grande pour y stocker du vin.** (+ adjective)
It's big enough to store some wine.

Il est *assez* **stressé en ce moment.** (+ adjective)
He's rather/quite stressed

C'est *trop* **loin du centre-ville.** (+ adverb)
It's too far away from the city centre.

Trop can be used with a verb to mean 'too much':

Il travaille *trop*.
He works too much.

You can use **assez de** and **trop de** in front of nouns. **Trop de** can
be used in front of nouns in the singular or the plural and is then
usually translated by 'too much' or 'too many'.

C'est *trop de* **travail pour une femme seule.**
It's too much work for a woman on her own.

J'ai acheté *trop de* **pommes.**
I've bought too many apples.

Il y a *assez de* **place pour installer un séchoir et une planche
à repasser.**
There's enough room to put a clothes-horse and an ironing
board.

Exercise 7

The French are famous for complaining about pretty much everything. Here are some likely complaints. Fill in the gaps with **assez (de)** or **trop (de)**.

1 J'ai _____ travail et pas _____ vacances.
2 Quel été pourri! Il ne fait pas _____ chaud et il pleut _____ .
3 C'est scandaleux! Tu as vu le salaire des joueurs de foot! Ils gagnent bien _____ argent et ils sont _____ médiocres.
4 Oh là, là, ça va pas, ce matin. J'ai bu _____ vin hier soir et j'ai _____ mangé.
5 Tu n'as pas acheté _____ pain. On est six et il n'y a qu'une baguette.

Exercise 8

Read the two ads. Do you think either of these two houses would interest Chantal and Jacques? Using some of the expressions you have learned to express your opinion and **assez (de)** and **trop (de)**, say what you think of the size of the houses, the number of bedrooms, the price, the location and what they have to offer.

MAISON DE VILLE

Surface habitable 70m²
1 chambre, salle de bains,
cuisine meublée, séjour
petite cour pavée 25m²
5 mn du centre-ville dans
quartier calme

prix: 100 000 Euros

MAISON DE CHARME

Surface habitable 200m²
4 chambres, 2 salles de
bains, cuisine, séjour
grand jardin de 600m² avec
pelouse et
vue sur lac
à 10 km de commerces

PRIX: **260 000 EUROS**

la pelouse lawn   **un lac** a lake

Example: **Je pense que la maison de ville est trop petite. Elle n'a qu'une chambre.**

17 On discute de la maison

Talking about the house

In this unit you will learn about:

- expressing wishes, preferences and obligation with the subjunctive
- talking about events in the past with **pendant**
- using verbs with and without a preposition
- using the pronouns **le, la, les** and **lui, leur**

Dialogue 1 🎧 (Audio 2; 46)

Coup de foudre

Jacques and Chantal are discussing Laure Breton's house. They both have fallen in love with it, but Jacques has some reservations.

CHANTAL: J'ai vraiment le coup de foudre pour cette maison!

JACQUES: Moi aussi. Mais j'aimerais qu'on réfléchisse bien avant de faire une offre. Je trouve qu'elle est assez chère. Tu as vu l'état de la cuisine et de la salle de bains?

CHANTAL: Oui, c'est vrai. Il faudrait qu'on fasse pas mal de travaux.

JACQUES: Il faut tout refaire et ça risque de coûter très cher.

CHANTAL: C'est sûr. Tu crois qu'on a les moyens?

JACQUES: Ben, il faut qu'on regarde notre budget de près. Je ne voudrais pas que nous ayons des problèmes d'argent. Je serai bientôt à la retraite et nous n'aurons pas autant de revenus. Je n'ai pas envie que tu ne puisses plus dépenser de petites fortunes dans les magasins! Je sais que tu adores ça!

CHANTAL: Tu sais bien que je suis raisonnable!

JACQUES: Je plaisantais! Mais, tu sais, ce n'est pas seulement la cuisine et la salle de bains qui sont très vétustes. Le toit a l'air d'avoir besoin de quelques réparations aussi.

CHANTAL: Oui, je crois que M. et Mme Breton ont négligé pas mal de choses pendant trop d'années.

JACQUES: J'ai aussi regardé l'état des planchers quand vous étiez en train de discuter de ses plantes, et c'est pas brilliant.

Vocabulary

le coup de foudre	love at first sight	**réfléchir**	to think
avant	before	**une offre**	offer
l'état	the state, the condition		
il faudrait	(conditional of **il faut**), (*here*) we would need to/ we would have to		
pal mal de	quite a lot of	**des travaux**	(building) work, alterations
avoir les moyens	to be able to afford	**des revenus**	income
vétuste	decrepit, showing its age	**les planchers**	wooden floors

Language points

Expressing wishes, preferences and obligation with the subjunctive

You already know how to use the following verbs expressing wishes, preferences or obligation with another verb in the infinitive.

J'aimerais (*bien/mieux*) **aller au cinéma.**
Il *voudrait* **devenir architecte.**

Nous *voulons* **acheter une maison.**
Nous *avons envie de* **faire du français.**

Je *préfère* aller au restaurant.
Il *faut* tout refaire.

You can use the verbs or expressions above followed by **que** (that) very much like the verbs **penser**, **croire** or **trouver** you encountered in the previous unit. Using **que** allows you to introduce another subject different from the one you are using with the first verb.

Compare the following two sets of sentences:

Je *pense changer* de travail.   (one subject throughout: **je**)
I am thinking of changing jobs.

Je *pense que tu as* raison.   (two subjects: **je** and **tu**)
I think (that) you are right.

Il *veut rester* à Paris.   (one subject: **il**)
He wants to stay in Paris.

Il *veut qu'elles travaillent* plus.   (two subjects: **il** and **elles**)
He wants them to work more.

Whenever you want to use verbs expressing *wishes* or *preferences* such as **vouloir**, **aimer**, **avoir envie**, **préférer** or when you want to use **falloir** (as in **il faut** or **il faudrait**) followed by **que**, the verb after **que** will be in a new form called the *subjunctive*. As you saw in the previous unit, this is generally not the case for **penser**, **croire** and **trouver**.

Using the *subjunctive* is not a refinement. All French people use it. Generally it is not difficult to use because it tends to come with specific verbs or expressions that you can easily memorise. In this course, you will only learn how to use it with **falloir** and verbs expressing *wishes* or *preferences*.

J'aimerais qu'on *réfléchisse* bien.
I would like us to think about it carefully.

Il *faudrait* qu'on *fasse* pas mal de travaux.
We would need to make quite a few alterations.

Il *faut* qu'on *regarde* notre budget de près.
We need/have to look at our budget closely.

Je ne *voudrais* pas que nous *ayons* des problèmes d'argent.
I would not like us to have money problems.

Je n'*ai* pas *envie* que tu ne *puisses* plus dépenser de petites fortunes dans les magasins!
I would not like you not to be able to spend a small fortune in the shops, anymore!

How to form the subjunctive

For most verbs, simply take out the **-ent** of the **ils/elles** form of the verb in the present tense and add to the stem (what's left of the verb) the following endings, as shown in the example with **partir**: **e**, **es**, **e**, **ions**, **iez**, **ent**.

   ils/elles partent   →   **part -ent**   →   **part** (stem)

The verb partir

que je part**e**   que nous part**ions**
que tu part**es**   que vous part**iez**
que il/elle/on part**e**   que ils/elles part**ent**

There are a few exceptions. Here are some you need to know. Look them up in the reference grammar at the end of the book: **aller**, **vouloir**, **pouvoir**, **faire**, **venir**, **être** and **avoir**.

Exercise 1 🎧 (Audio 2; 47)

Fill in the gaps with the correct form of the verb in brackets.

1 Il faut que nous _____ (partir) de bonne heure.
2 Je voudrais que tu _____ (venir) avec moi.
3 J'aimerais mieux qu'ils _____ (faire) leur travail.
4 Elle ne veut pas que vous _____ (finir) tard.
5 Il faudrait que nous _____ (avoir) plus de temps.

Exercise 2

Infinitive or **que** + subjunctive? Translate the following sentences.

1 I want you to come with us.
2 She needs to buy some butter.
3 He would like to go on holiday.
4 We'd rather he looks for a job.
5 They have to buy another house.

Exercise 3

Annie is not happy with her 18-year-old son. Make her talk to him taking the example as a model. Use verbs expressing wishes and preferences as well as **il faut** or **il faudrait**.

> *Example*: **ranger la chambre** (tidy up the bedroom)
> **J'aimerais que tu ranges ta chambre.**

1 travailler plus à l'école

2 sortir moins souvent avec des amis

3 faire moins de bruit après 11 heures du soir

4 manger plus sainement et boire moins

5 arrêter de fumer dans les toilettes

Language points

Talking about events in the past with pendant

You can use **pendant** + *duration* (e.g. **deux heures**, **trois mois**, **quelques années**, etc.) to say for how long an event went on in the past. **Pendant** is then normally translated by 'for' in English. The tense of the verb used in French will normally be the **passé composé**. The event you are talking about is over.

> **M. et Mme Breton ont négligé pas mal de choses *pendant* trop d'années.**
> M. et Mme Breton neglected quite a few things for too many years.

> **J'ai attendu le train *pendant* quatre heures.**
> I waited for the train for four hours.

> ***Pendant* des siècles, on a cru que le soleil tournait autour de la terre.**
> For centuries, it was believed that the sun revolved around the earth.

Exercise 4

Make sentences following the example.

Example: **Elle   travailler   vingt ans**
Elle a travaillé pendant vingt ans.

1 Paul   dormir   trois heures
2 Nous   fumer   des années
3 Il   pleuvoir   tout le mois le juillet
4 Tu   travailler   combien de temps?
5 Je   ne pas faire de sport   dix ans

Dialogue 2 🎧 (Audio 2; 48)

L'offre

*Jacques and Chantal have finally made an offer on the house through
Mme Duclos' estate agency. As they have not had an answer yet,
Chantal rings Mme Duclos.*

MME DUCLOS: Oui, allô, Mme Duclos à l'appareil.
CHANTAL: Bonjour, ici c'est Chantal Mercier. Mon mari et
               moi avons fait une offre sur la maison de Mme
               Breton. Vous avez des nouvelles? Vous lui avez
               parlé?
MME DUCLOS: Oui, alors, je lui ai téléphoné tout de suite après
               votre appel pour lui communiquer votre offre.
CHANTAL: Et toujours pas de réponse?
MME DUCLOS: Non, pas pour l'instant. J'ai essayé de la rappeler
               hier et ce matin, mais ça ne répond pas. Je suis
               débordée aujourd'hui mais, attendez. J'ai deux
               collègues qui font visiter une maison pas loin de
               chez elle. Je peux leur demander de passer la voir,
               si vous voulez.
CHANTAL: C'est vraiment gentil. Mon mari et moi attendons
               sa réponse avec impatience. Nous sommes tombés
               sous le charme de cette maison. Notre offre est
               peut-être un peu basse, mais il y a beaucoup de
               travaux à faire. Qu'est-ce que vous en pensez?

MME DUCLOS: Oui, je lui ai dit que son prix est trop élevé. J'ai vu la maison, il y a un mois ou deux et je la trouve adorable mais je pense qu'elle a bien besoin de quelques rénovations. Vous voulez que je demande à Mme Breton de vous contacter directement pour discuter de votre offre?

CHANTAL: Euh, écoutez, je préfère que nous traitions avec vous.

MME DUCLOS: D'accord. Ne vous inquiétez pas. Je m'en occupe et je vous appelle le plus tôt possible.

Vocabulary

avoir des nouvelles	to have news	**tout de suite**	straight away
après	after	**un appel**	phone call
une réponse	an answer	**répondre**	to answer
faire visiter	to show around	**tomber sous le charme**	to fall under the spell
bas(se)	low	**élevé**	high
traiter	to treat; (*here*) to deal with		

Language points

Using verbs with and without a preposition

In Unit 11, you learned how to recognise a **direct object**. More often than not, a verb in French will be followed by its object(s). Objects can be **direct** or **indirect**. It depends on whether or not the verb used with its object(s) is followed by a preposition or not.

When the verb used with its object(s) is not followed by a preposition, we have a **direct object** construction.

Elle *écoute* les informations tous les soirs.   (direct)
She listens to the news every evening.

Mon mari et moi *attendons* sa réponse avec impatience.   (direct)
My husband and I are waiting for her answer impatiently.

When the verb used with its object(s) is followed by a preposition (such as **à**), we have an *indirect object* construction. Though there are others, the most common preposition used in French is normally **à**.

> **Elle *téléphone* à ses amis de temps en temps.**   (indirect)
> She phones her friends now and again.

> **Vous voulez que je *demande* à Mme Breton de vous contacter?**   (indirect)
> Do you want me to ask Mme Breton to contact you?

Exercise 5

Direct or indirect object constructions?

1 Elle parle à sa sœur.
2 Tu invites Marc, ce soir?
3 J'ai vu les amis de Sandra.
4 J'écris rarement à mes collègues.
5 Vous avez demandé à qui?
6 Vous allez contacter qui?
7 A qui est-ce qu'elle dit bonjour?
8 Elle a donné rendez-vous à Mme Breton.
9 A qui tu envoies cette lettre?

Exercise 6

How often do you stay in contact with the following people? Make sentences, using the verbs provided.

> *Example*: **vos amis**
> **J'appelle mes amis tous les jours.**

1 vos parents
2 vos frères et vos sœurs
3 votre meilleur ami(e)
4 vos enfants

> téléphoner   parler   appeler   voir
> écrire   contacter   inviter

Language points

Using the pronouns le, la, les *and* lui, leur

In Unit 14, you came across the pronouns **le**, **la**, and **les** and used them to avoid the repetition of things previously mentioned.

> **L'apéritif, on *le* prend sur la terrasse?**

You can also use **le**, **la**, **les** to talk about people.

> **J'ai essayé de *la* rappeler hier.　(Mme Breton)**
> I tried to ring her again yesterday.

> **Patrick? Non je ne *le* vois pas aujourd'hui.　(Patrick)**
> Patrick? No, I'm not seeing him today.

> **Ils invitent ses parents souvent?**
> **Oui, ils *les* invitent tous les dimanches.　(ses parents)**
> Does he invite his parents often?
> Yes, he invites them every Sunday.

Le, **la**, **les** are only used in *direct object construction*. This is why they are called *direct object pronouns*.

le　replaces someone male/something masculine singular

la　replaces someone female/something feminine singular

les　replaces more than one person (male or female)/something in the plural

Remember that **le** and **la** will become **l'** in front of a word starting with a vowel or an '**h**'.

　　Lui, **leur** are also pronouns but unlike **le**, **la**, **les** they are are only used to talk about people (and animals). And because they are only used in *indirect object construction* (generally with **à**), they are called *indirect object pronouns*.

> **Vous *lui* avez parlé?　(à Mme Breton)**
> Did you talk to her?

> **Je peux *leur* demander de passer la voir.**
> **(à mes deux collègues)**
> I can ask them to go and see her.

lui   replaces someone male or female

leur replaces more than one person (male or female)

Both the *direct object pronouns* **le**, **la**, **les** and the *indirect object pronouns* **lui**, **leur** are generally placed before the verb they are linked with.

As you can see, 'him' can be translated by **le** or **lui**, 'her' by **la** or **lui**, and 'them' by **les** or **leur**, depending on the verb you are using them with.

But what about 'me', 'you', 'us'?

Regardless of the verb you use them with, 'me', 'you' and 'us' are always translated by the same word.

Il *me* parle souvent.	**Je *te* téléphone.**
He talks to me often.	I'll phone you.
Il *nous* regarde manger.	**Je vais *vous* expliquer.**
He is watching us eat.	I'm going to explain (it) to you.

So, to summarise, here is the full list of *direct* and *indirect object pronouns*:

Direct object pronouns	Indirect object pronouns
me	me
te	te
le, la	lui
nous	nous
vous	vous
les	leur

Did you notice?

When you use **lui** or **leur** with a verb in the **passé composé**, the past participle does not agree in gender and number with the noun(s) **lui** or **leur** replace.

Je *lui* ai téléphoné tout de suite après votre appel.
  (à **Mme Breton**)

Je *leur* ai téléphoné, mais ils ne sont pas là.
(à **mes parents**, for example)

Exercise 7

Fill in the gaps with **le**, **la**, **l'**, **les**, **lui** or **leur**.

1 J'ai vu Pierre hier et je _____ ai parlé de toi.

2 J'ai invité Martha à manger. Tu _____ connais?

3 Les enfants vont au lit. Tu vas _____ raconter une histoire?

4 Il n'est toujours pas là. Je _____ attends depuis une heure!

5 Vous avez rendez-vous avec M. Mercier? Je _____ contacte tout de suite.

6 Je viens de _____ téléphoner, mais ils ne sont pas encore rentrés.

7 Appelle-la et dis-_____ de venir tout de suite dans mon bureau.

Exercise 8

Coup de foudre! Bernard has just met a woman he's fallen in love with instantly and is making plans. Using direct and indirect object pronouns, the verbs listed below and verbs expressing wishes, make sentences, following the example. Refer back to the language points of this unit for guidance.

Example: **Il voudrait *lui* donner rendez-vous.**

**parler   inviter au restaurant   téléphoner
écrire   dire   épouser**

Do the same for Danielle who has fallen in love with a man she has not spoken to yet.

18 Négociations

Negotiations

In this unit you will learn about:

- reporting what someone is saying
- some formal forms of address

Dialogue 1 🎧 (Audio 2; 50)

On négocie

Chantal is phoning Jacques at work to tell him that Mme Breton has refused their offer on the house.

CHANTAL: Jacques? C'est moi. Je viens d'avoir Mme Duclos au téléphone. Elle dit que Mme Breton a refusé notre offre.

JACQUES: Je m'en doutais. Bon, je pense qu'on peut monter un peu plus. On en discutera ce soir.

CHANTAL: C'est à dire que Mme Duclos pense que Mme Breton a reçu une offre directe d'autres personnes intéressées. Elle me demande si nous voulons faire une nouvelle offre.

JACQUES: Est-ce que Mme Duclos a pu parler à Mme Breton?

CHANTAL: Oui et elle pense que nous devons agir vite si nous voulons la maison. Apparemment Mme Breton dit qu'elle veut obtenir le prix qu'elle demande pour faire la vente.

JACQUES: 150 000 euros!

CHANTAL: Oui.

JACQUES: Tu sais qu'il y a au moins 10 000 euros de travaux pour remettre la cuisine et la salle de bains en état?

CHANTAL:	Oui, je sais bien. Mais elle est fabuleuse, cette maison. Mme Duclos me demande de lui téléphoner le plus vite possible si nous voulons faire une nouvelle offre. Qu'est-ce qu'on fait alors?
JACQUES:	Demande-lui si Mme Breton accepterait 140 000 euros. Tu peux lui dire que les travaux pour refaire la cuisine et la salle de bains coûteront au moins 10 000 euros. Et puis, je ne suis pas très content que Mme Breton traite avec d'autres acheteurs potentiels en même temps!
CHANTAL:	Moi non plus. Je trouve que ce n'est pas très correct.
JACQUES:	Bon, on fait comme ça, alors?
CHANTAL:	Oui, très bien. Et si elle refuse encore?
JACQUES:	Dans ce cas-là, on lui offrira le prix qu'elle demande.

Vocabulary

je m'en doutais	I thought so, I'm not surprised	**agir**	to act
apparemment	apparently	**remettre en état**	to renovate
un acheteur	buyer		

Language points

Reporting somebody else's words

You can report what someone says in different ways.

- When reporting a *statement*, the verb used is usually **dire**. Note the use of **que**.

  Mme Duclos says: 'Mme Breton a refusé votre offre.' Her words are reported by Chantal in this way:

  Elle dit que **Mme Breton a refusé notre offre.**
  She says that Mme Breton has refused our offer.

  Mme Breton says: 'Je veux obtenir le prix que je demande.' Chantal reports her words to Jacques in this way:

  *Mme Breton dit qu'***elle veut obtenir le prix qu'elle demande.**
  Mme Breton says that she wants to obtain the asking price.

Jacques says: 'Les travaux pour refaire la cuisine et la salle de bains coûteront au moins 10 000 euros.' He suggests reporting his words in this way:

> ***Tu peux lui dire que* les travaux pour refaire la cuisine et la salle de bains coûteront au moins 10 000 euros.**
> You can tell her that the work on the kitchen and bathroom will cost at least 10 000 euros.

* When reporting a *question* answered by yes or no, the verb used is normally **demander**. Note the use of **si**.

Mme Duclos asks: 'Vous voulez faire une nouvelle offre?' Her question is reported by Chantal in this way:

> ***Elle* me *demande si* nous voulons faire une nouvelle offre.**
> She asks me if we want to make a new offer.

Jacques wants Chantal to ask: 'Est-ce que Mme Breton accepterait 140 000 euros?' He says to Chantal:

> ***Demande*-lui *si* Mme Breton accepterait 140 000 euros.**
> Ask her if Mme Breton would accept 140 000 euros.

* When reporting *a request made in the imperative*, the verbs used are usually **demander** or **dire.** Note that they are then followed by **de** + *verb in the infinitive*.

Mme Duclos says: 'Téléphonez-moi le plus vite possible.' Chantal reports her words in this way:

Mme Duclos me *demande de* lui *téléphoner* le vite possible.
Mme Duclos asks me to phone her as quickly as possible.

Marie says to her son: 'Rentre avant minuit.' You can report her speech like this.

Elle lui *dit de rentrer* avant minuit.
She tells him to come back before midnight.

Exercise 1

Here are sentences reporting what people are saying or have just said. Following the example, find their own words.

Example: **Bernard dit qu'il est fatigué.**
'Je suis fatigué.'

1 Pierre dit qu'il fait beau à Paris.
2 Elle demande à son mari d'acheter le journal.
3 Eric demande à Sylvie si elle veut aller au cinéma.
4 Jacques dit que la maison est trop chère.
5 Mes parents me demandent si je viens les voir cet été.

Exercise 2

Now report the following words.

1 'Il pleut tous les jours.'
   Elle dit _____ .

2 'Pierre part en vacances?'
   Il me demande _____ .

3 'Passe à la banque.'
   Elle te dit _____ .

4 'Je viens de gagner un million à la Loterie.'
   Il dit _____ .

5 'Jacques et Chantal vont acheter cette maison?'
   Ils te demandent _____ .

Dialogue 2 🎧 (Audio 2; 52)

On va signer

Mme Duclos leaves a message on Jacques and Chantal's answer-phone.

JACQUES: Vous êtes sur le répondeur de M. et Mme Mercier. Nous sommes absents pour le moment. Veuillez, s'il vous plaît, laisser un message ou nous rappeler plus tard.

MME DUCLOS: M. et Mme Mercier? C'est Mme Duclos à l'appareil. Je suis ravie de vous dire que Mme Breton a accepté votre offre de 140 000 euros. Je me permets de vous suggérer de contacter votre notaire rapidement pour signer l'acte de vente le plus vite possible. Je sais que Mme Breton souhaite partir en vacances la semaine prochaine. Si vous voulez bien fixer un rendez-vous avec votre notaire et me communiquer la date et l'heure, je me mettrai en contact avec Mme Breton. Merci et bonne soirée.

Vocabulary

le répondeur	answering machine	**laisser**	to leave
absent	(*here*) not at home	**un notaire**	solicitor
signer	to sign	**l'acte de vente**	contract of sale

Language points

Some formal forms of address

The French can be quite formal in some situations. You might find the following expressions useful.

> *Je suis ravi(e) de* **vous dire que Mme Breton a accepté votre offre.**
> I am delighted to tell you that Mme Breton has accepted your offer.

Je me permets de **vous suggérer de contacter votre notaire rapidement.**
May I suggest you get in touch with your solicitor quickly?

Si vous voulez bien **fixer un rendez-vous avec votre notaire ...**
If you could arrange a meeting with your solicitor ...

Veuillez **s'il vous plaît, laisser un message ou nous rappeler plus tard.**
Please leave a message or call us again later.

Other useful expressions are:

Je suis vraiment navré(e) de **vous annoncer que vous avez échoué à votre examen.**
I am really sorry to have to tell you that you have failed at your examinations.

Je vous remercie de **votre cadeau.**
I thank you for your present.

Je vous prie de **m'envoyer vos tarifs.**
Please send me your list of prices.

And if you need to end a formal letter to someone you don't know personally, here are two formulae you could use:

Veuillez agréer, Monsieur, l'expression de mes sentiments les meilleurs.

Je vous prie de croire, Madame, à l'assurance de mes salutations distinguées.

There are endless variations on these two examples above, but all can be translated by 'yours sincerely' or 'yours faithfully'.

However, you can use something shorter if, for example, you send an email:

Veuillez recevoir mes sincères salutations.
Sincères salutations.

Exercise 3

You need to record a voicemail message on your French answering machine. Read Jacques's message again and using it as a model, write your own message and say it out loud. Include the following information:

1 say the caller has reached your answerphone
2 say you are not at home
3 ask the caller to please leave his/her name and phone number
4 say you'll call him/her later

Exercise 4

Paul Dupré is planning to renovate his kitchen. He has received an estimate from M. Duras, a local builder, and is now answering him by email. Fill in the gaps in Paul's email with some of the expressions you have just learned.

M. Duras,

(1) _____ de nous répondre si rapidement. Ma femme et moi (2) _____ d'accepter votre devis. (3) _____ , s'il vous plaît, nous contacter prochainement. Nous aimerions fixer une date le plus rapidement possible.

(4) _____

Paul Dupré

Exercise 5

Les Anglais envahissent la France

NON CE N'EST pas le début d'une nouvelle guerre de cent ans mais un phénomène qui inquiète pas mal les Français. Après la Côte d'Azur, la Dordogne, la Normandie et le Périgord, les Britanniques découvrent et colonisent toutes les régions françaises. Ils sont partout, achètent des fermes en mauvais état que personne ne veut, font monter le prix des terrains et des maisons à un rythme inquiétant et ouvrent même des pubs et magasins qui proposent des produits anglais comme la *Marmite*®, le chocolat *Cadbury*®, des *beans* dans une sauce orange horriblement sucrée . . .

Les Britanniques seraient plus de 600 000 à posséder une résidence en France. Certains y habitent de manière permanente, d'autres y viennent pour les vacances seulement. Parce que les prix de l'immobilier sont franchement exorbitants de l'autre côté de la Manche, les Britanniques peuvent se permettre d'acquérir en France de petits châteaux ou de grandes propriétés pour le prix d'une maison de banlieue chez eux.

Read this text a couple of times. You will not understand everything but look out for words you understand to get a general idea of what it is about. Then answer the questions.

1 Who is the text talking about?
2 What are they doing?
3 Where are they doing it?

Now, read the first paragraph again and say which of the following are mentioned.

4 the Hundred Years' War
5 the health of the French
6 four French regions
7 derelict farms
8 villas
9 the price of land and houses
10 pubs and shops offering British products

Read the second paragraph and find in the text the equivalent to the following:

11 à avoir une maison en France
12 sont vraiment excessivement élevés
13 en Grande-Bretagne
14 ont la possibilité d'acheter

Reference grammar

Numbers

0	zéro	25	vingt-cinq
		26	vingt-six
1	un	27	vingt-sept
2	deux	28	vingt-huit
3	trois	29	vingt-neuf
4	quatre	30	trente
5	cinq	31	trente et un
6	six	32	trente-deux ...
7	sept		
8	huit	40	quarante ...
9	neuf	50	cinquante ...
10	dix	60	soixante ...
11	onze	70	soixante-dix
12	douze	71	soixante et onze
13	treize	72	soixante-douze
14	quatorze	73	soixante-treize
15	quinze	74	soixante-quatorze
16	seize	75	soixante-quinze
17	dix-sept	76	soixante-seize
18	dix-huit	77	soixante-dix-sept
19	dix-neuf	78	soixante dix-huit
		79	soixante-dix-neuf
20	vingt		
21	vingt et un	80	quatre-vingts
22	vingt-deux	81	quatre-vingt-un
23	vingt-trois	82	quatre-vingt-deux
24	vingt-quatre	83	quatre-vingt-trois

84	quatre-vingt-quatre	92	quatre-vingt-douze
85	quatre-vingt-cinq	93	quatre-vingt-treize
86	quatre-vingt-six	94	quatre-vingt-quatorze
87	quatre-vingt-sept	95	quatre-vingt-quinze
88	quatre-vingt-huit	96	quatre-vingt-seize
89	quatre-vingt-neuf	97	quatre-vingt-dix-sept
		98	quatre-vingt-dix-huit
90	quatre-vingt-dix	99	quatre-vingt-dix-neuf
91	quatre-vingt-onze		

100	cent
101	cent un
200	deux cents
201	deux cent un
1000	mille
10 000	dix mille
100 000	cent mille
1 000 000	un million

Gender and number

Nouns in French are either maculine or feminine. Because gender is carried by the noun, it affects words around it, such as articles and adjectives.

The mark of the feminine for an adjective is usually an **-e**. There are exceptions. The most useful ones are listed in Unit 7.

The mark of the plural for both nouns and adjectives is usually an **-s**. Again there are exceptions.

Nouns ending in **-au**, **-eau** and **-eu** normally have an **-x** in the plural:

un chapeau   **des chapeaux**
un feu   **des feux**

Nouns ending in **-al** normally have their plural in **-aux**:

un cheval   **des chevaux**

Negative sentences

Negative words such as **ne ... pas**, **ne ... jamais**, **ne ... plus** or **ne ... rien** are usually placed on either side of the verb:

Il *n'*aime *pas* le café.
Elle *ne* travaille *jamais*.

Il *n'*est *plus* venu.
Ils *ne* veulent *rien* faire.

Questions

Questions are usually formed in two ways:

Tu veux venir?	(rising intonation)
Est-ce que **tu veux venir?**	(using **est-ce que**)
Vous venez quand?	(rising intonation)
Quand *est-ce que* **vous venez?**	(using **est-ce que**)

Verbs and tenses

The present tense

Nearly all verbs have the following endings:

Je	e	*or*	s
Tu	es	*or*	s
Il	e	*or*	t
Nous	ons		
Vous	ez		
Ils	ent		

Exceptions include: **être**, **avoir**, **faire**, **aller**, **pouvoir**, **vouloir** and verbs ending in **-dre**.

Most verbs ending in **-er** follow the **chercher** model. For other verbs, there are other models. We have provided the most useful models below. The list is by no means exhaustive but provides you with a good starting point.

Model		*Other verbs*
chercher		all verbs in **-er** apart from **aller** and the verbs in **-er** below
je cherch e	nous cherch ons	
tu cherch es	vous cherch ez	
il cherch e	ils cherch ent	
préférer		all verbs in **é + consonant + -er**
je préfèr e	nous préfér ons	
tu préfèr es	vous préfér ez	
il préfèr e	ils préfèr ent	
(se) promener		all verbs in **e + consonant + -er** such as **acheter** apart from those following the **appeler** model
je promèn e	nous promen ons	
tu promèn es	vous promen ez	
il promèn e	ils promèn ent	
appeler		and **rappeler, épeler**; this is the normal model for verbs in **-eler** and **-eter** though some follow the **promener** model
j'appell e	nous appel ons	
tu appell es	vous appel ez	
il appell e	ils appell ent	
manger		all verbs in **-ger**
je mang e	nous mang eons	
tu mang es	vous mang ez	
il mang e	ils mang ent	
placer		all verbs in **-cer**
je plac e	nous plaç ons	
tu plac es	vous plac ez	
il plac e	ils plac ent	
essayer		**payer** is the other one you have encountered in the course
j'essai e *or* j'essay e	nous essay ons	
tu essai es *or* tu essay es	vous essay ez	
il essai e *or* il essay e	ils essai ent *or* ils essay ent	

Model		*Other verbs*
envoyer		all other verbs in **-yer** such as **appuyer**
j'envoi e	nous envoy ons	
tu envoi es	vous envoy ez	
il envoi e	ils envoi ent	
aller		and **ouvrir, couvrir, découvrir**
je vais	nous all ons	
tu vas	vous all ez	
il va	ils vont	
offrir		
j'offr e	nous offr ons	
tu offr es	vous offr ez	
il offr e	ils offr ent	
dormir		and **(re)partir, (res)sentir, servir, (re)sortir, mentir**
je dor s	nous dorm ons	
tu dor s	vous dorm ez	
il dor t	ils dorm ent	
venir		**tenir** and all compounds of **tenir** and **venir** such as **revenir, devenir, se souvenir, obtenir**
je vien s	nous ven ons	
tu vien s	vous ven ez	
il vien t	ils vienn ent	
lire		and **interdire, cuire, conduire, produire, traduire**
je li s	nous lis ons	
tu li s	vous lis ez	
il li t	ils lis ent	
écrire		and all verbs in **-crire** such as **prescrire, décrire**
j'écri s	nous écriv ons	
tu écri s	vous écriv ez	
il écri t	ils écriv ent	

Model		*Other verbs*
finir		**agir** is the other one you have come across
je fini s	nous finiss ons	
tu fini s	vous finiss ez	
il fini t	ils finiss ent	
dire		
je di s	nous dis ons	
tu di s	vous dit es	
il di t	ils dis ent	
voir		and **prévoir**
je voi s	nous voy ons	
tu voi s	vous voy ez	
il voi t	ils voi ent	
savoir		
je sai s	nous sav ons	
tu sai s	vous sav ez	
il sai t	ils sav ent	
devoir		and all verbs in **-evoir** such as **concevoir**
je doi s	nous dev ons	
tu doi s	vous dev ez	
il doi t	ils doiv ent	
pouvoir		and **vouloir**
je peu x	nous pouv ons	
tu peu x	vous pouv ez	
il peu t	ils peuv ent	
avoir		
j'ai	nous av ons	
tu as	vous av ez	
il a	ils ont	

Model		*Other verbs*
boire		
je boi s	nous buv ons	
tu boi s	vous buv ez	
il boi t	ils boiv ent	
croire		
je croi s	nous croy ons	
tu croi s	vous croy ez	
il croi t	ils croi ent	
faire		and its compounds
je fai s	nous fais ons	
tu fai s	vous faites	
il fai t	ils font	
connaître		and **naître**
je connai s	nous connaiss ons	
tu connai s	vous connaiss ez	
il connaî t	ils connaiss ent	
attendre		and **défendre, descendre, entendre, prendre, répondre, vendre, perdre**
j'attend s	nous attend ons	
tu attend s	vous attend ez	
il attend	ils attend ent	
prendre		and compounds such as **apprendre, comprendre**
je prend s	nous pren ons	
tu prend s	vous pren ez	
il prend	ils prenn ent	
suivre		and **vivre**
je sui s	nous suiv ons	
tu sui s	vous suiv ez	
il sui t	ils suiv ent	

Model		*Other verbs*
mettre		and compounds such as **promettre**
je met s	nous mett ons	
tu met s	vous mett ez	
il met	ils mett ent	
être		
je suis	nous sommes	
tu es	vous êtes	
il est	ils sont	

The passé composé

This tense is formed by conjugating **avoir** or **être** in the present tense and adding the past participle form of the verb you want to use. Most verbs use **avoir**.

All reflexive verbs and a few other verbs listed below use **être**.

Verbs using **être**: **naître**, **mourir**, **aller**, **venir**, **entrer**, **sortir**, **arriver**, **partir**, **retourner**, **monter**, **descendre**, **passer**, **rester**, **devenir**, **tomber** and all their compounds such as **revenir**.

finir	**venir**
j'ai fini	je suis venu(e)
tu as fini	tu es venu(e)
il a fini	il est venu
nous avons fini	nous sommes venu(e)s
vous avez fini	vous êtes venu(e)(s)
ils ont fini	ils sont venus

Useful past participles

All verbs ending in **-er** have their past participle in **-é**; others don't. Here is a list of the most useful:

attendre	attendu	mourir	mort
avoir	eu	offrir	offert
boire	bu	ouvrir	ouvert
conduire	conduit	partir	parti
connaître	connu	plaire	plu
construire	construit	pleuvoir	plu
croire	cru	pouvoir	pu
cuire	cuit	prendre	pris
découvrir	découvert	recevoir	reçu
descendre	descendu	répondre	répondu
devenir	devenu	rire	ri
devoir	dû	sentir	senti
dire	dit	servir	servi
dormir	dormi	sortir	sorti
écrire	écrit	suivre	suivi
entendre	entendu	tenir	tenu
être	été	vendre	vendu
faire	fait	venir	venu
falloir	fallu	vivre	vécu
interdire	interdit	voir	vu
lire	lu	vouloir	voulu
mettre	mis		

The imperfect or l'imparfait

This tense is easily formed by using the **nous** form of the present tense of the verb. Simply remove the **-ons** ending and use the remaining stem throughout the conjugation, adding the endings: **-ais**, **-ais**, **-ait**, **-ions**, **-iez**, **-aient**.

Example:

vendre   **nous** *vend* **-ons**

---

vendre

---

je vend**ais**
tu vend**ais**
il vend**ait**
nous vend**ions**
vous vend**iez**
ils vend**aient**

The simple future

With most verbs, the simple future uses for its stem the part of the
infinitive that comes before the **r**. For instance the stem for **aimer**
will be **aime-** and for **vendre** it will be **vend-**. You simply then add
the endings: **-rai**, **-ras**, **-ra**, **-rons**, **-rez**, **-ront**.

---

descendre

---

je descend**rai**
tu descend**ras**
il descend**ra**
nous descend**rons**
vous descend**rez**
ils descend**ront**

Some verbs have an irregular stem. Here are the most useful ones:

être	→	se-	→	je serai
avoir	→	au-	→	j'aurai
faire	→	fe-	→	je ferai
pouvoir	→	pour-	→	je pourrai
vouloir	→	voud-	→	je voudrai
devoir	→	dev-	→	je devrai
aller	→	i-	→	j'irai
venir	→	viend-	→	je viendrai
voir	→	ver-	→	je verrai
falloir	→	faud-	→	il faudra
savoir	→	sau-	→	je saurai

The conditional

The conditional uses exactly the same stem as the simple future. The list of verbs with an irregular stem is the same as for the simple future. The endings for the conditional are: **-rais**, **-rais**, **-rait**, **-rions**, **-riez**, **-raient**.

descendre	
je descend**rais**	nous descend**rions**
tu descend**rais**	vous descend**riez**
il descend**rait**	ils descend**raient**

The subjunctive

For most verbs, simply remove the **-ent** from the **ils/elles** form of the verb in the present tense and add to the stem the following endings as shown in the example with partir: **-e**, **-es**, **-e**, **-ions**, **-iez**, **-ent**.

Example:

partir   **Ils** *part* **-ent**

partir	
que je part**e**	que nous part**ions**
que tu part**es**	que vous part**iez**
qu'il part**e**	qu'ils part**ent**

Here are a few exceptions:

avoir	**être**
que j'aie	que je sois
que tu aies	que tu sois
qu'il ait	qu'il soit
que nous ayons	que nous soyons
que vous ayez	que vous soyez
qu'ils aient	qu'ils soient

aller	faire
que j'aille	que je fasse
que tu ailles	que tu fasses
qu'il aille	qu'il fasse
que nous allions	que nous fassions
que vous alliez	que vous fassiez
qu'ils aillent	qu'ils fassent

vouloir	pouvoir
que je veuille	que je puisse
que tu veuilles	que tu puisses
qu'il veuille	qu'il puisse
que nous voulions	que nous puissions
que vous vouliez	que vous puissiez
qu'ils veuillent	qu'ils puissent

venir

que je vienne
que tu viennes
qu'il vienne
que nous venions
que vous veniez
qu'ils viennent

The imperative

It has only three persons (**tu**, **nous** and **vous**). For most verbs, it is similar to the present tense. For all verbs ending in **-er**, there is no 's' in the **tu** form except when the verb is followed by **en** or **y**.

Chercher

cherche
cherchons
cherchez

But:

Cherches-en! **Vas-y!**

For **avoir** and **être** the imperative is similar to the subjunctive.

avoir	être
aie	sois
ayons	soyons
ayez	soyez

Key to exercises

Unit 1

Exercise 1

1 êtes, suis; 2 sont; 3 est; 4 sommes; 5 es; 6 est

Exercise 2

1 Non, elle est américaine.
2 Non, il est russe.
3 Non, elle est française.
4 Non, il est espagnol.
5 Non, je suis anglais/anglaise. (for example)

Exercise 3

1 Non, elle est écossaise.
2 Non, elle habite à Coventry.
3 Non, elle travaille à Londres.
4 Oui, elle parle français.
5 Non, je suis anglais(e), etc.

Exercise 6

2 (a); 4 (b); 1 (c); 3 (d)

Quel est votre nom? Quelle est votre nationalité? Quelle est votre adresse? Quel est votre numéro de téléphone? Quelle est votre profession?

Exercise 7

You may have answered:

1 Je ne suis pas français(e).
2 Je n'habite pas à Lille.
3 Je ne travaille pas à Londres.
4 Je parle anglais.
5 Je ne suis pas journaliste.

Unit 2

Exercise 1

Both are masculine. The article **un** gave the gender away.

1 une; 2 un; 3 un; 4 un salon de coiffure; 5 La; 6 Le; 7 le; 8 Le

Exercise 2

Il y a une piscine, un restaurant, un sauna, un bar, un fax, un salon de coiffure?

Vous avez une piscine, un restaurant, un sauna, un bar, un fax, un salon de coiffure?

Exercise 3

1 Oui, le fax est au deuxième étage.
2 C'est au deuxième étage aussi.
3 Oui, la salle de gym est au premier étage.
4 C'est au rez-de-chaussée.
5 Oui, le restaurant est au rez-de-chaussée.
6 C'est au sous-sol.

Exercise 4

Excusez-moi, je cherche **la** pharmacie, s'il vous plaît.
Excusez-moi, pour aller **à** la pharmacie, s'il vous plaît.
Excusez-moi, je cherche **le** château, s'il vous plaît.
Excusez-moi, pour aller **au** château, s'il vous plaît.
[etc.]

Exercise 5

La mairie, c'est loin? Non, c'est à 1 kilomètre.
L'aéroport, c'est loin? Non, c'est à 12 kilomètres.
Le théâtre, c'est loin? Non, c'est à 2 minutes en voiture.
[etc.]

Exercise 6

1 allez, tournez; 2 continuez; 3 prenez; 4 est; 5 à gauche; 6 la deuxième rue à droite; 7 tout droit; 8 à gauche; 9 à droite; 10 allez à droite; 11 continuez; 12 tournez; 13 est

Exercise 7

1 Vous allez tout droit. Et puis, vous prenez la deuxième rue à droite. La pharmacie est à droite.
2 Pour la gare. Vous continuez tout droit et vous tournez à gauche. La gare est à droite.

Exercise 8

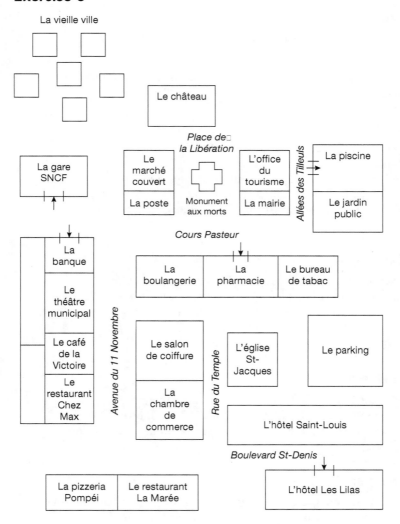

Unit 3

Exercise 1

Nouns in the plural are: **tranches**, **amandes**, **fromages**, **desserts**, **pommes**, **glaces**, **sorbets**.

Dans la salade printanière, il y a des artichauts, des tomates, des asperges, des oignons et des carottes.

Exercise 2

1 C'est vrai.
2 C'est faux. Juliette déteste les moules.
3 C'est faux. Elle n'aime pas beaucoup le poisson sauf le thon.
4 C'est faux. Elle aime beaucoup les desserts.

Exercise 3

Here are a few sample answers:

J'adore le chocolat mais je déteste le poisson. J'aime bien les tomates mais je n'aime pas du tout les épinards.

Exercise 4

1 J'aime bien les escargots mais je préfère les huîtres.
2 J'aime beaucoup les glaces mais je préfère la tarte aux pommes.
3 J'aime bien le poulet mais je préfère le poisson.
4 J'adore le steak tartare, mais je préfère le thon.

Exercise 5

1 Qu'est ce que c'est, une assiette de crudités?
2 Qu'est ce que c'est, un carpaccio de bœuf?
3 Qu'est ce que c'est, le Ricard®?
4 Qu'est ce que c'est, une assiette de charcuterie?

1 (d); 2 (b); 3 (a); 4 (c)

(i) C'est une sélection de légumes crus: tomates, carottes, céleri
     . . .
(ii) C'est des tranches fines de bœuf cru.
(iii) C'est un alcool au parfum d'anis.
(iv) C'est des tranches de charcuterie: saucisson, jambon, pâté . . .

Exercise 6

1 prenez; 2 prends; 3 prends; 4 prends; 5 prennent; 6 Qu'est-ce que c'est, une menthe à l'eau?; 7 Je prends une menthe à l'eau, alors.

Exercise 7

1 Vous travaillez à Londres? Oui, et vous?
3 Tu prends un café? Oui, et toi?

Exercise 8

1 à; 2 à; 3 aux; 4 d'; 5 de

Unit 4

Exercise 1

1 infirmière
2 chef cuisinier
3 Ils sont employés de banque.
4 Elle est chanteuse.
5 Il est journaliste.
6 Elle est étudiante.

Exercise 2

1 Elle n'est pas mariée. Elle est célibataire.
2 Ils ne sont pas divorcés. Ils sont mariés.
3 Il n'est pas retraité.
4 Je suis marié(e), célibataire, divorcé(e).

Exercise 3

1 Charles a 30 ans.
2 Christine a 24 ans.
3 J'ai + number + ans.

Exercise 4

Because of française and mariée, you should have guessed that
Claude is a woman.

1 c; 2 d; 3 a; 4 e; 5 b

Exercise 5

Il s'appelle Christian Dufresne. Il est français. Il a 54 ans. Il est
marié. Il a 2 enfants. Natasha a 28 ans et Emilie a 34 ans. Il est
acteur.

Elle s'appelle Daniella Cecaldi. Elle est italienne. Elle a 38 ans.
Elle est célibataire. Elle n'a pas d'enfants. Elle est directrice de
marketing.

Exercise 6

1 fait; 2 allons; 3 allez; 4 fais; 5 vais; 6 fait; 7 font

Exercise 7

Here a few possible answers:

1 Nous faisons du jogging. Vous faites du squash. Tu fais de l'équitation.
2 Marie et Chantal vont à l'hôpital. Jacques va à la piscine. Je vais au centre-ville. Vous allez aux Etats-Unis.
3 The verb used twice is **jouer**:
   Je **joue au** golf.
   Il **joue aux** échecs.

Exercise 8

J'adore lire. Je déteste faire le ménage. J'aime regarder la télévision.
   [etc.]

Exercise 9

1 Faux. Jacques est représentant pour une société informatique.
2 Vrai et faux. Ils n'habitent pas à Limoges.
3 Vrai.
4 Faux. Chantal et Jacques ont un fils et une fille.
5 Faux. Jacques n'est pas sportif mais Chantal adore faire de l'exercice. Elle est très sportive.
6 Vrai.
7 Faux. Jacques aime aller à la pêche.

Unit 5

Exercise 1

1 vont passer; 2 vont louer; 3 va louer; 4 va aller; 5 vont prendre

Exercise 2

1 Vrai.
2 Faux. Ils ne vont pas louer un petit studio en Sicile.
3 Faux. Anne ne va pas passer deux ou trois jours à Limoges.
4 Vrai.
5 Faux. Jacques et Chantal n'ont pas l'intention de louer une voiture pour le week-end.

Exercise 3

1 en; 2 en; 3 en; 4 Au; 5 au; 6 le; 7 au; 8 en; 9 en; 10 en; 11 aux; 12 à; 13 en; 14 en; 15 en

Exercise 4

1 Oui, on va à Paris.
2 Non, on ne travaille pas en France.
3 Oui, on va faire du yoga.
4 Non, on n'a pas l'intention de visiter la Thaïlande.

Exercise 5

Je voudrais/j'aimerais prendre des vacances en octobre.
Je voudrais/j'aimerais louer un camping-car.
Je voudrais/j'aimerais travailler à Londres/au cinéma.
Je voudrais/j'aimerais visiter les arènes d'Arles.
Je voudrais/j'aimerais aller au cinéma/à Londres.
Je voudrais/j'aimerais faire du karaté.

Exercise 6

1 Je pars le 28 juin et je rentre le 12 juillet.
2 Je pars le 30 octobre et je rentre le 5 novembre.
3 Je pars le vendredi 25 décembre et je rentre le mardi 30.
4 Je pars le lundi 3 février et je rentre le jeudi 6.

Exercise 7

1 35 euros per day
2 45 euros per day
3 All taxes included (TTC: Toutes taxes comprises)
4 It's only available from 10 July to 20 August inclusive, and you must book on the internet.
5 Bonjour madame/monsieur. Je voudrais louer une voiture pour sept jours, du 21 au 28 août.

Unit 6

Exercise 1

Ils ont du lait, du pain, du beurre, de l'eau minérale, du café, de la mayonnaise, de la moutarde, du dentifrice, de l'huile et du vinaigre.

Exercise 2

Il nous faut de l'huile, du vinaigre, du sel et du poivre. Nous avons besoin de Coca®, de jus d'orange, de lessive et de viande.

Exercise 3

1 Où se trouve l'eau minérale, s'il vous plaît?
2 Excusez-moi, je cherche le rayon papeterie.
3 Où se trouve le rayon des surgelés, s'il vous plaît?
4 Excusez-moi, je cherche la mayonnaise.
5 Où se trouve le sel, s'il vous plaît?
6 Excusez-moi, je cherche le rayon des conserves.

Exercise 4

2; 3; 4; 7; 8

Exercise 5

Here's an example of what you could have said:

- Je voudrais un kilo de tomates et une livre d'abricots, s'il vous plaît.
- J'aimerais 200 grammes de cerises et 2 avocats.
- Donnez-moi un peu de persil, s'il vous plaît.
- Je voudrais 4 tranches de thon et 300 grammes de crevettes.
- Et donnez-moi deux truites, s'il vous plaît.

Exercise 6

1 J'ai du vin./Je n'ai pas de vin.
2 J'ai de la moutarde./Je n'ai pas de moutarde.
3 J'ai de l'eau minérale./Je n'ai pas d'eau minérale.
4 J'ai du café./Je n'ai pas de café.
5 J'ai des chips./Je n'ai pas de chips.
6 J'ai des yaourts./Je n'ai pas de yaourts.
7 J'ai du lait./Je n'ai pas de lait.
8 J'ai du thon./Je n'ai pas de thon.

Exercise 8

1 (d); 2 (c); 3 (a); 4 (b); 5 (e)

Unit 7

Exercise 1

1 Faux; 2 Faux; 3 Vrai; 4 Faux; 5 Vrai; 6 Vrai; 7 Vrai; 8 pouvez;
9 sais; 10 peut; 11 peux; 12 savons; 13 peuvent

Exercise 2

1 Je dois faire des courses. 2 Je dois aller au restaurant avec Anne.
3 Je ne peux pas. Je dois partir.

Exercise 3

1 arrive; 2 part, arrive; 3 part, 14 h 55, arrive, 17 h 39

Exercise 4

1 Faux. L'avion est plus cher que le train.
2 Faux. Le train de 10 h 34 est plus rapide.
3 Faux. Il est plus cher.
4 Faux. Il est moins pratique et il est moins cher.

Exercise 5

1 anglaise; 2 bon; 3 petit; 4 australiens; 5 rapide

Exercise 6

1 Elle part quand?/Quand est-ce qu'elle part?
2 Vous allez/tu vas où, au mois de juillet?/Où est-ce que vous allez/tu vas au mois de juillet?
3 Ça coûte combien?/Combien est-ce que ça coûte?
4 Ils invitent qui?/Qui est-ce qu'ils invitent?
5 Le train part à quelle heure?/A quelle heure est-ce que le train part?
6 Marie veut acheter quoi?/Qu'est-ce que Marie veut acheter?

Exercise 7

Here is an example of questions you could have asked:

– A quelle heure est-ce qu'il y a un train pour Nice?
– Où est-ce que je dois changer?
– A quelle heure est-ce que le train arrive à Marseille?
– A quelle heure est-ce que je pars de Marseille?
– A quelle heure est-ce que le train arrive à Nice?

Unit 8

Exercise 1

1 ai mangé; 2 a fait; 3 avons joué; 4 avez pris; 5 ont acheté; 6 as visité; 7 a eu

Exercise 2

Elle a pris un taxis. Elle a oublié sa valise dans le taxi. Elle a appelé la compagnie de taxis. Ils ont trouvé le chauffeur tout de suite.

Exercise 3

1 Je n'ai pas mangé au restaurant.
2 Il n'a pas fait de courses.
3 Nous n'avons pas joué au tennis.
4 Vous n'avez pas pris le train?
5 Ils n'ont pas acheté de sofa.
6 Tu n'as pas visité le musée Grévin?
7 On n'a pas eu de problème.

Exercise 4

Il a réservé une place dans le TGV pour Paris. Il a annulé les réunions pour mardi. Il n'a pas réservé une table à la pizzeria Stromboli. C'est fermé. Il a envoyé la facture de M. Dubois. Il n'a pas organisé une réunion avec Mme Toulet. Elle est en vacances.

Exercise 5

1 onze heures et quart (du soir)
2 deux heures et demie (de l'après-midi)
3 onze heures cinq (du matin)
4 quatre heures moins dix (de l'après-midi)
5 midi
6 deux heures moins le quart (de l'après-midi)

Exercise 6

1 Ahmed est le père de Nedim.
2 Clara est la fille de Gina.
3 Malika est la nièce de Nedim.
4 Nasser est le frère de Malika.
5 Clara est la cousine de Malika.
6 Nedim est l'oncle de Julie.
7 Jean-Pierre est le grand-père de Benjamin.

Exercise 7

1 C'est ...
  (a) ma fille; (b) mon fils; (c) ma belle-fille

2 C'est ...
  (a) mon frère; (b) mon neveu; (c) mes parents

3 C'est ...
  (a) son père; (b) ses sœurs; (c) sa grand-mère

Exercise 8

1 ce, ce; 2 Cet; 3 Cette; 4 ces; 5 cette, ce

Exercise 9

1 A married couple with children
2 They want a good job first and enjoy being single
3 Single-parent families (*monoparentales*) or where one or both parents have been married before and have children from their previous marriage(s) (*recomposées*).
4 It's easier to get a divorce and start a new life. Living together outside marriage is not taboo any more.
5 They choose not to live with their partner.
6 Matthieu
7 Cécile
8 Théo
9 Hélène
10 Maximilien

Unit 9

Exercise 1

1 man; 2 woman; 3 man; 4 woman; 5 man; 6 woman; 7 one person (man); 8 group of people; 9 one person (woman); 10 group of women; 11 group of people

Exercise 2

1 Tim et Sandra sont allés au cinéma.
2 Il n'est pas resté au lit.
3 Elle est retournée à Paris.
4 Anna est devenue journaliste.
5 Malika et Anne sont restées dans un hôtel, une nuit.

Exercise 3

Bernard et Françoise sont arrivés à Nice le 10 juillet. Ils sont restés dans un petit hôtel. Ils ont visité des musées et des monuments. Ils sont allés à Cannes et à Saint-Tropez. Ils ont pris des photos. Ils sont rentrés à Paris le 22 juillet.

Exercise 4

1 nous levons; 2 s'amuse; 3 vous souvenez de; 4 me repose; 5 se promènent; 5 te maries

Exercise 5

Je me lève à midi tous les jours. Je me promène dans le parc. Je me repose. Je m'occupe de mes enfants et je m'amuse avec eux. Je me couche très tard.

Exercise 6

1 woman; 2 man; 3 woman; 4 man; 5 woman; 6 man

Exercise 7

Il s'est levé à 11h tous les jours. Il s'est promené sur la plage le matin. Il s'est reposé l'après-midi. Il ne s'est pas couché tard. Il s'est ennuyé un peu.

Exercise 8

Chère Christine,

Je suis arrivée à Marseille. Je me suis promenée dans la ville et je suis allée à la plage. Je me repose bien. Je mange au restaurant tous les soirs! C'est vraiment des vacances!

Bises

Malika

Exercise 9

1 Malika vient en Angleterre en juillet.
2 Est-ce que vous venez/tu viens jouer au golf dimanche?
3 Elle vient d'arriver à Paris.
4 Nous venons de voir un bon film à la télévision.
5 Ils viennent de partir.

Exercise 10

1 Non merci, je viens de manger.
2 Je suis fatigué, je viens de jouer au tennis.
3 Desolé, elle vient de partir.
4 Je n'ai pas le temps, je viens de rentrer de vacances.

Exercise 11

1 Il ne fait rien.
2 Nous ne jouons plus au golf.
3 Ils ne travaillent jamais.
4 Elles n'ont rien trouvé.
5 Vous n'avez plus de monnaie.
6 Elle ne va jamais au théâtre.
7 Je n'habite plus à Paris.

8 Je n'ai plus d'argent.
9 Oui, il est à la retraite mais il ne fait rien.
10 Ils n'ont rien trouvé.
11 Je ne vais jamais au cinéma.
12 Elle ne fait jamais la cuisine.

Unit 10

Exercise 1

1 On pourrait sortir prendre un verre.
2 On pourrait aller au cinéma.
3 On pourrait partir en week-end.
4 On pourrait se reposer.
5 On pourrait se promener dans Montmartre.

Exercise 2

Je préférerais/j'aimerais mieux . . .

1 visiter le musée de Cluny.
2 me reposer.
3 regarder la télévision.
4 aller à l'hôtel.
5 rester célibataire.

Exercise 3

1 Oui, j'y reste deux nuits.
2 Oui, elles y vont avec des amis.
3 Oui, j'y suis allé(e) l'an dernier.
4 Oui, elles y sont.
5 Oui, ils y sont allés.
6 Non, je n'y reste pas deux nuits.
7 Non, elles n'y vont pas avec des amis.
8 Non, je n'y suis pas allé(e) l'an dernier.
9 Non, elles n'y sont pas.
10 Non, ils n'y sont pas allés.

Exercise 4

Aujourd'hui, il fait beau. Il y a du soleil mais il y a du vent. Il fait
bon. Hier, il a plu et il a neigé. Il a fait froid.

Exercise 5

1 Montparnasse est/est situé/se trouve au sud-ouest du centre.
2 Versailles est/est situé/se trouve au sud-ouest de Paris.

3 Le bois de Boulogne est/est situé/se trouve à l'ouest de Paris.
4 . . . au nord-ouest du centre.
5 . . . au nord-ouest du centre.
6 . . . à l'est du centre.

Exercise 6

1 Le Sacré-Cœur, c'est une basilique qui est située/se trouve au nord.
2 La Défense est un quartier qui est situé/se trouve au nord-ouest de Paris.
3 Versailles est un château qui est situé/se trouve au sud-ouest de Paris.
4 Le Louvre est un musée qui est situé/se trouve dans le centre de Paris.
5 Le Centre Pompidou est un bâtiment moderne qui est situé/se trouve dans le centre de Paris.

Exercise 7

On peut monter en haut de la tour et on voit toute la ville. On peut aussi se balader dans les petites rues de la ville. On mange très bien dans les restaurants indiens et on peut aller boire des bières traditionnelles dans les pubs.

Exercise 8

1 Le touriste y trouve tout le charme du vieux Paris.
2 un remarquable panorama sur Paris.
3 on peut se balader des heures et des heures dans les petites rues pittoresques et les escaliers.
4 multiples terrasses de café et les chevalets des peintres qui cherchent à faire fortune.
5 le mot russe 'bistro' (...) amené par les occupants russes au début du 19ᵉ siècle.
6 la rue Saint-Rustique a neuf siècles et a conservé ses pavés (cobble stones) et son caniveau central.

Unit 11

Exercise 1

1 Elle a l'air en pleine forme.
2 Il a l'air heureux.
3 Il a l'air stressé.
4 Ils ont l'air en colère.

Exercise 2

Answers will vary but you might have used the following:

- Elle se lève à dix heures.
- Il s'habille.
- Il ne se couche pas.
- Elle se couche à minuit, etc.

Exercise 3

Answers will vary but you might have used the following:

Je me lève à huit heures et je me couche à onze heures.
Le week-end dernier, je me suis levé(e) à dix heures et je me suis couché(e) à minuit.

Exercise 4

Here are some sample answers:

1 Tu devrais/vous devriez faire un régime.
2 Tu devrais te/vous devriez vous reposer.
3 Tu devrais/vous devriez acheter une maison en France.
4 Tu devrais/vous devriez faire un peu d'exercice.

Exercise 5

1 Il travaille en France depuis sept ans.
2 Elle s'occupe des enfants depuis la semaine dernière.
3 Ils sont en vacances depuis deux semaines, maintenant.
4 Il travaille avec eux depuis Noël.

Exercise 6

4 (a); 6 (b); 1 (c); 2 (d); 3 (e); 5 (f)

Exercise 7

1 Couchez-vous; 2 Faites; 3 Partez; 4 Prenez, revenez

Unit 12

Exercise 1

1 venions; 2 partait; 3 faisais; 4 devaient; 5 avais; 6 pouvait;
7 vouliez; 8 étions

Exercise 2

1 était; 2 rentrions; 3 roulions; 4 était; 5 commençait; 6 avons vu; 7 nous sommes arrêtés; 8 sommes descendus; 9 avait; 10 regardait; 11 a dit; 12 s'est enfui

Exercise 3

Il ne faisait vraiment pas beau. La radio et le chauffage ne marchaient pas. Le coffre ne fermait pas bien et il pleuvait à l'intérieur de la voiture. Il y avait un camion devant eux. Jacques ne pouvait pas doubler parce que le camion roulait assez vite. Et tout à coup, le pare-brise de la voiture a éclaté.

Exercise 4

- Il est resté au lit toute la journée parce qu'il ne se sentait pas bien.
- La route est fermée à cause d'un accident.
- Il est parti de bonne heure parce qu'il avait un rendez-vous chez un client.
- Il ne voyait pas grand-chose à cause du brouillard.

Exercise 5

1 La vie est plus dure.
2 On voyage plus facilement.
3 Je travaille aussi rapidement/vite.
4 Mon dessert est meilleur.
5 Je vais/pars en vacances moins souvent.
6 C'est mieux.

Exercise 6

1 plus de, moins
2 autant, plus
3 moins d', plus de
4 plus, plus de

Exercise 7

Here's a sample answer:

On avait moins d'argent et on travaillait plus. On voyageait moins, mais on communiquait plus souvent. On avait moins de confort, mais on était moins stressé. On était plus heureux. Il y avait moins de pollution, mais autant de guerres!

Exercise 8

1 l'hôtel Raymond; 2 l'hôtel du Parc; 3 l'hôtel Raymond; 4 l'hôtel Raymond; 5 l'hôtel Raymond

Unit 13

Exercise 1

1 viendrons; 2 partira; 3 feras; 4 devront; 5 aurai; 6 pourra; 7 prendrez; 8 serons

Exercise 2

1 Tu rencontreras l'homme/la femme de ta vie.
2 Vous aurez cinq enfants.
3 Vous gagnerez un million à la loterie.
4 Vous arrêterez de travailler.
5 Vous achèterez plusieurs maisons en France.
6 Vous vivrez très longtemps.

Exercise 3

You may have answered like this:

1 Tu devrais prendre des vacances.
2 J'aimerais mieux/je préférerais rester à la maison.
3 On pourrait aller au cinéma.
4 Je voudrais un thé.
5 Est-ce que je pourrais parler à un détective, s'il vous plaît?

Exercise 4

Your dialogue could look like this:

THOMAS: Quand est-ce que vous pouvez venir?
JULIETTE: Je suis disponible lundi après-midi et mardi matin.
THOMAS: Alors, voyons. Je suis en réunion lundi après-midi.
            Ah et malheureusement je suis en déplacement mardi
            matin. Je vais voir des clients à Avignon. Quel
            dommage! Et puis après, je suis en congés.
JULIETTE: Attendez! Je pourrais peut-être trouver un moment
            lundi en fin de matinée. Je suis très occupée mais
            je devrais être libre vers 11 heures. Ça vous con-
            viendrait?
THOMAS: C'est parfait.

Exercise 5

1 Je viendrai à la plage avec vous s'il ne pleut pas.
2 Je viendrai avec vous si je ne finis pas trop tard au travail.
3 Je viendrai avec vous si je ne suis pas fatigué(e).
4 Je viendrai avec vous si je peux prendre des congés.
5 Je viendrai avec vous si je suis libre.

Exercise 6

Here are some sample answers:

Si je gagnais à la loterie, j'achèterais une belle voiture.
J'arrêterais de travailler. Je partirais vivre en France ...

Exercise 7

1 Si on allait visiter un musée?
2 Si tu prenais des vacances?
3 Si on allait au restaurant?
4 Si on allait au cinéma?
5 Si tu allais te coucher?

Exercise 8

1 sera; 2 voudrait/veut; 3 appellera; 4 aimerait, avait; 5 appellera, finit

Unit 14

Exercise 1

1 coupes les courgettes ...
2 tu alternes une rangée de courgettes ...
3 Tu mélanges les œufs au lait.
4 Tu ajoutes une pincée de sel ...
5 tu verses la mixture ...
6 Tu mets au four ...
7 Tu laisses cuire une heure.

Exercise 2

1 le four
2 les courgettes et les tomates
3 les œufs
4 le mélange
5 le flan de légumes; le flan de légumes

6   le petit déjeuner, le bus, etc.
7   la télévision, la météo, etc.
8   les clés, les mains, etc.
9   les mauvais souvenirs, les devoirs, etc.
10 une lettre, une liste, etc.

Exercise 3

1 le; 2 la; 3 les; 4 l'; 5 les; 6 la

Exercise 4

1   Oui, je l'ai vu.
2   Oui, on la fait.
3   Oui, je les ai trouvées.
4   Non, je ne l'ai pas entendue.
5   Oui, je l'ai pris.
6   Oui, je le taperai.
7   Non, je ne les ai pas mises à la boîte.

Exercise 5

1   Oui, j'en prends.
2   Oui, j'en achèterai.
3   Non, je n'en veux pas.
4   Non, je n'en mange pas souvent.
5   Oui, nous en avons acheté.

Exercise 6

1   J'en ai une douzaine.
2   Oui, j'en ai trois.
3   Oui, j'en ai une.
4   Non, je n'en ai pas.
5   Oui, j'en ai beaucoup.

Exercise 7

1   Mets-le sur la table.
2   Prenons un taxi.
3   Achetez-en un peu.
4   Laisse-les dans le barbecue.
5   Allons-y tout de suite.
6   Fais-la pour demain.
7   Sois gentil avec elle.
8   Ne la laisse pas toute seule.

Exercise 8

1 Coupe les courgettes ...
2 alterne une rangée de courgettes ...
3 Mélange les œufs au lait.
4 Ajoute une pincée de sel ...
5 verse la mixture ...
6 Mets au four ...
7 Laisse cuire une heure.

Unit 15

Exercise 1

1 yellow; 2 red; 3 green; 4 brown; 5 violet, purple

And then: 1 (h); 2 (f); 3 (c); 4 (i); 5 (j); 6 (k); 7 (d); 8 (a); 9 (l); 10 (b); 11 (e); 12 (g)

Exercise 2

1 en vert; 2 en velours; 3 en soie; 4 en cuir; 5 en coton; 6 en jaune

Exercise 3

1 J'adore le rouge.
2 Je voudrais des chaussettes noires.
3 J'aime bien ces gants. Vous les avez en marron?
4 Il a acheté un blouson en cuir.
5 Vous avez cette jupe en S?
6 J'aime bien cette chemise bleue mais je préfère la rose.

Exercise 4

1 celle-ci/celle-là
2 lequel/celui-ci, celui-là
3 celui-ci/celui-là
4 Lesquelles
5 ceux-ci/ceux-là

Exercise 5

1 Elle n'achète que des marques de grands couturiers.
2 Elle ne va qu'à des concerts de grands musiciens.
3 Le dimanche midi, elle ne mange que du caviar et ne boit que du champagne.
4 Elle n'achète que des modèles de luxe.

And you may have answered:

5 Elle n'a que des amis riches.
6 Elle n'aime que les sports chers.
7 Il n'aime que les films d'action.
8 Il n'achète que des pantalons noirs.
9 Il n'aime que le poulet et les frites.
10 Il n'écoute que du jazz.

Exercise 6

1 (c); 2 (d); 3 (a); 4 (b)

Exercise 7

1 Je ne veux rien, merci.
2 Il n'aime personne.
3 Vous cherchez quelque chose?
4 J'ai vu quelqu'un.
5 Ils ne trouvent jamais rien dans ce magasin.

Exercise 8

1 going for a walk, travelling, going to exhibitions and museums, accepting invitations to dine out, going to nightclubs and bars, eating out.
2 It's a secondhand market
3 became more widespread
4 No. It's a fake.
5 He knows because he owns a home decoration shop selling the same item.

Unit 16

Exercise 1

1 que; 2 qui; 3 qui; 4 où; 5 qui; 6 que; 7 où

Exercise 2

1 Les oranges sont des fruits d'hiver qui sont riches en vitamine C.
2 *La Chute* est un roman de Camus que j'aime beaucoup.
3 La Loire est une région magnifique où on trouve d'excellents vins blancs doux.
4 François Mitterrand était un homme politique contesté qui avait ses partisans.
5 C'est Patrick que j'ai rencontré en vacances en Italie.

Exercise 3

Here are some sample answers:

1 Je pense qu'ils sont pratiques.
2 Je crois que c'est bien mais cher.
3 Je trouve que c'est souvent très cher.
4 Je crois que c'est une bonne idée.
5 A mon avis, c'est essentiel.

Exercise 4

1 il sera à la retraite
2 elle sera à Paris
3 referons le jardin
4 seront grands
5 pourrai téléphoner

Exercise 5

1 dans; 2 il y a; 3 Il y a; 4 dans; 5 Dans; 6 il y a

Exercise 6

You may have answered:

1 Il y a une antenne sur le toit.
2 Il y a un jardin derrière la maison.
3 Il y a une terrasse devant la maison.
4 Il y a une cour derrière la maison.
5 Il y a une cave au-dessous de la cuisine.
6 Il y a un grenier sous le toit.
7 Il y a une buanderie derrière la cuisine.

Exercise 7

1 trop de, assez de; 2 assez, trop; 3 trop d', assez/trop; 4 trop de,
trop; 5 assez de

Exercise 8

Here is a sample answer:

Je trouve que la maison de ville est trop petite. Elle n'a qu'une
chambre. Il n'y a pas assez de place, à mon avis. Il n'y a pas de
jardin aussi.
    Je pense que la maison de charme est trop chère. Il y a trop
de chambres. Elle est peut-être aussi trop loin des commerces.
Je crois que le jardin est aussi trop grand.

Unit 17

Exercise 1

1 partions; 2 viennes; 3 fassent; 4 finissiez; 5 ayons

Exercise 2

1 Je veux que vous veniez/tu viennes avec nous.
2 Il faut qu'elle achète du beurre.
3 Il voudrait partir en vacances.
4 Nous aimerions mieux qu'il cherche un travail.
5 Il faut qu'ils achètent une nouvelle maison.

Exercise 3

Here is what you might have said:

1 Je voudrais que tu travailles plus à l'école.
2 J'aimerais que tu sortes moins souvent avec tes amis.
3 Il faut que tu fasses moins de bruit après 11 heures du soir.
4 J'aimerais que tu manges plus sainement et que tu boives moins.
5 Il faudrait aussi que tu arrêtes de fumer dans les toilettes.

Exercise 4

1 Paul a dormi pendant trois heures.
2 Nous avons fumé pendant des années.
3 Il a plu pendant tout le mois le juillet.
4 Tu as travaillé pendant combien de temps?
5 Je n'ai pas fait de sport pendant dix ans.

Exercise 5

1 indirect; 2 direct; 3 direct; 4 indirect; 5 indirect; 6 direct;
7 indirect; 8 direct and indirect: donner **rendez-vous à**; 9 direct
and indirect: envoyer **une lettre à**

Exercise 6

Here are some sample answers:

1 Je téléphone à/parle à/appelle/invite mes parents tous les week-
ends.
2 J'écris à/parle à/contacte/invite mes frères et mes sœurs une fois
par semaine.

3 Je vois mon/ma meilleur(e) ami(e) tous les jours.
4 Je parle à/invite/contacte mes enfants très souvent.

Exercise 7

1 lui; 2 la; 3 leur; 4 l'; 5 le; 6 leur; 7 lui

Exercise 8

Here are some sample answers:

Il/Elle voudrait lui donner rendez-vous. Il/elle aimerait lui parler et l'inviter au restaurant. Il/elle voudrait aussi lui téléphoner et lui écrire pour lui dire: 'Je t'aime.' Et, évidemment, il/elle aimerait bien l'épouser.

Unit 18

Exercise 1

1 'Il fait beau à Paris.'
2 'Achète le journal.'
3 'Tu veux aller au cinéma?'
4 'La maison est trop chère.'
5 'Tu viens nous voir cet été?'

Exercise 2

1 Elle dit qu'il pleut tous les jours.
2 Il me demande si Pierre part en vacances.
3 Elle te dit de passer à la banque.
4 Il dit qu'il vient de gagner un million à la Loterie.
5 Ils te demandent si Jacques et Chantal vont acheter cette maison.

Exercise 3

Vous êtes sur le répondeur de X. Je suis absent(e) pour le moment. Veuillez, s'il vous plaît, laisser votre nom et votre numéro de téléphone. Je vous rappellerai plus tard.

Exercise 4

1 Je vous remercie; 2 sommes ravis; 3 Veuillez; 4 Sincères salutations

Exercise 5

1 British people
2 Buying properties
3 In France
4, 6, 7, 9 and 10 are mentioned.
11 à posséder une résidence en France
12 sont franchement exorbitants
13 de l'autre côté de la Manche, chez eux
14 peuvent se permettre d'acquérir

French–English glossary

A

à côté de	next to
abord (d')	first
abricot (m.)	apricot
absent	absent
absolument	absolutely
accepter	to accept
acheter	to buy
acheteur, -euse	buyer
acrylique (m.)	acrylic
acte de vente (m.)	contract of sale
acteur, actrice	actor, actress
actif	active
actuel	present, current
adolescence (f.)	adolescence
adorable	adorable
adorer	to love
adresse (f.)	address
aéroport (m.)	airport
affaires (d')	business
affectueusement	fondly
âge (m.)	age
agence immobilière (f.)	estate agency
agir	to act
agriculteur (m.)	farmer
aider	to help
aimer	to love, like
air (avoir l')	to look, seem
ajouter	to add

alcool (m.)	alcohol
aller	to go
aller-retour (m.)	round trip, return ticket
allumer	to light
alors	then, so
alterner	to alternate
amandes (f.)	almonds
américain	American
ami (m.)	friend
amicalement	best wishes
amitiés	best wishes
amuser (s')	to have fun
ananas (m.)	pineapple
anglais	English
année (f.)	year
annonce (f.)	advertisement
annuler	to cancel
antenne (f.)	aerial
août (m.)	August
apéritif (m.)	aperitif
apéro (m.)	aperitif
appareil (à l')	on the phone
apparemment	apparently
appel (m.)	call
appeler (s')	to call, be called
appuyer	to push, put pressure
après	after
après-midi (m., f.)	afternoon
architecte (m.)	architect

arènes (f.)	amphitheatre	**bas**	low
argent (m.)	money, silver	**bateau** (m.)	boat
argentin	Argentine	**bâtiment** (m.)	building
arrêter (**s'**)	to stop	**beau**	beautiful
arrivée (f.)	arrival	**beaucoup**	a lot
arriver	to arrive	**beau-fils** (m.)	son-in-law
arriver à	to manage,	**beau-frère** (m.)	brother-in-law
	succeed in	**beau-père** (m.)	father-in-law
artichaut (m.)	artichoke	**belge**	Belgian
ascenseur (m.)	lift	**belle-fille** (f.)	daughter-in-law
asperge (f.)	asparagus	**belle-mère** (f.)	mother-in-law
assez	enough	**belle-sœur** (f.)	sister-in-law
assiette (f.)	plate	**besoin** (**avoir**)	to need
assurance (f.)	insurance	**beurre** (m.)	butter
atelier (m.)	workshop	**bien**	well
attenant	adjoining	**bien sûr**	of course
attendre	to wait	**bière** (f.)	beer
attentif	attentive	**billet** (m.)	note, ticket
au revoir	goodbye	**biscuit** (m.)	biscuit
aubergine (f.)	aubergine	**bise** (f.)	kiss
au-dessous	underneath,	**bisou** (m.)	kiss
	below	**blanc**	white
au-dessus	above	**bleu**	blue
aujourd'hui	today	**blouson** (m.)	jacket
aussi	too, as	**bœuf** (m.)	beef
australien	Australian	**boire**	to drink
autant	as much, as	**bois** (m.)	wood(s)
	many	**boîte** (f.)	tin, box
automne (m.)	autumn	**bon**	good
avant	before	**bonjour** (m.)	hello
avion (m.)	plane	**bonsoir** (m.)	good evening
avis (**à mon**)	in my opinion	**bord** (m.)	bank
avocat (m.)	avocado	**bordeaux** (m.)	burgundy
avoir	to have	**botte** (f.)	bunch
avril (m.)	April	**bouger**	to move
		bouillir (**faire**)	to boil
B		**boulangerie** (f.)	baker's
		bouteille (f.)	bottle
balader (**se**)	to go for a walk	**boutique** (f.)	shop, boutique
banque (f.)	bank	**bras** (m.)	arm
bar (m.)	bar	**bricolage** (m.)	DIY
barbecue (m.)	barbecue	**bricoler**	to do DIY

bricoleur (être) — to be good at DIY
bridge (m.) — bridge
brilliant — brilliant
brouillard (m.) — fog
bruit (m.) — noise
brûler (se) — to burn (oneself)
buanderie (f.) — utility room
budget (m.) — budget
buffet (m.) — sideboard
bus (m.) — bus

C

cabaret (m.) — cabaret
café (m.) — coffee, café
caisse (f.) — checkout
calme — quiet
camion (m.) — lorry
campagne (f.) — countryside
camping-car (m.) — camping car
canard (m.) — duck
caractère (m.) — character
carnet (m.) — notebook
carotte (f.) — carrot
carte (f.) — card
carte de crédit (f.) — credit card
casser (se) — to break
catégorie (f.) — category
cause de (à) — because of
cave (f.) — cellar
caviar (m.) — caviar
ce, cette — this, that
célèbre — famous
céleri (m.) — celery
célibataire — single
celle-ci, celle-là — this one, that one
celles-ci, celles-là — these ones, those ones
celui-ci, celui-là — this one, that one

cendre (f.) — ash
centime (m.) — cent
centre-ville (m.) — city centre
céréale (f.) — cereals
cerise (f.) — cherries
certains — some
ces — these, those
ceux-ci, ceux-là — these ones, those ones
chaise (f.) — chair
chaleur (f.) — heat
chambre (f.) — bedroom
champagne (m.) — champagne
chance (f.) — luck
changer — to change
chanteur, -euse — singer
chapeau (m.) — hat
charbon de bois (m.) — charcoal
charcuterie (f.) — cooked meats
charme (m.) — charm
chat (m.) — cat
château (m.) — castle
chaud — hot
chauffeur, -euse — driver, chauffeur
chaussettes (f.) — socks
chaussures (f.) — shoes
chef (m.) — chef
cheminée (f.) — fireplace, chimney
chemise (f.) — shirt
chèque (m.) — cheque
cher — dear, expensive
chercher — to look for
cheville (f.) — ankle
chez — at, to
chien (m.) — dog
chips (m.) — crisps
chocolat (m.) — chocolate
choisir — to choose
choix (m.) — choice
chose (f.) — thing

ciel (m.) — sky
cimetière (m.) — cemetery
citron (m.) — lemon
clé (f.) — key
client, -e — customer, client
club (m.) — club
Coca® (m.) — Coke
cœur (m.) — heart
coffre (m.) — boot
cognac (m.) — brandy
coiffer (**se**) — to do one's hair
coiffeur, -euse — hairdresser
coiffure (f.) — hair style
collègue (m., f.) — colleague
combien — how much, how many
comme — like, as
commencer — to start
comment — how
commerce (m.) — business, businesses
commodités (f.) — facilities
communiquer — to communicate
compagnie (f.) — company
comprendre — to understand
comptable (m., f.) — accountant
concert (m.) — concert
conduire — to drive
conférence (f.) — conference
confirmer — to confirm
confiture (f.) — jam
confortable — comfortable
congé (m.) — annual leave
connaissance (f.) — acquaintance, knowledge
connaître — to know
conseil (m.) — advice
conserves (f.) — tinned, preserved food
construire — to build
contacter — to contact
continuer — to continue

contrarié — annoyed
contre (**par**) — on the other hand
convenir — to be convenient
copain, copine — friend, mate
correct — correct
côte (f.) — coast, rib
côté (m.) — side
coton (m.) — cotton
coucher (**se**) — to go to bed
couleur (f.) — colour
coup de foudre (m.) — love at first sight
couper (**se**) — to cut (oneself)
cour (f.) — yard
courgette (f.) — courgette
courses (**faire des**) — to shop
cousin, -e — cousin
coûter — to cost
couturier (**grand**) (m.) — clothes designer
couvert — indoor
crème (f.) — cream
crevé — shattered
crevette (f.) — prawn
croire — to believe
croisière (f.) — cruise
cru — raw
crudités (f.) — raw vegetables
cuillère (f.) — spoon
cuir (m.) — leather
cuire (**faire**) — to cook
cuisine (f.) — kitchen, cooking
cuisiner — to cook
cumin (m.) — cumin

D

dans — in
danser — to dance
date (f.) — date

débordé	snowed under with work	**diriger**	to run, be in charge of
début (m.)	beginning	**discuter**	to talk about
décembre (m.)	December	**disponible**	available, free
décoration (f.)	decoration	**distributeur** (m.)	cash machine
délicieux	delicious	**divorcé**	divorced
demain	tomorrow	**docteur** (m.)	doctor
demander	to ask	**document** (m.)	document
demi	half	**dommage** (**quel**)	what a shame
dent (f.)	tooth	**donc**	so
dentifrice (m.)	toothpaste	**donner**	to give
départ (m.)	departure	**dormir**	to sleep
dépendre	to depend	**dos** (m.)	back
dépenser	to spend	**double**	double
déplacement (**en**)	business trip (on)	**doucher** (**se**)	to shower
déplacer (**se**)	to move around	**douter** (**se**)	to have an inkling
depuis	since, for	**droit** (**tout**)	straight (on)
dernier	last	**droite** (**à**)	right (on the)
derrière	behind	**du, de la**	some, any
des	some	**dur**	hard
descendre	to go down		
désolé	sorry	**E**	
dessert (m.)	dessert		
détective (m., f.)	detective	**eau** (f.)	water
détester	to hate	**échecs** (m.)	chess
deuxième	second	**éclater**	to shatter
devant	in front	**école** (f.)	school
devenir	to become	**écossais**	Scottish
deviner	to guess	**écouter**	to listen
devoir	to owe, have to, must	**également**	also
différent	different	**église** (f.)	church
difficile	hard, difficult	**électro-ménager** (m.)	household electrical products
digestion (f.)	digestion	**élevé**	high
dimanche (m.)	Sunday	**embrasser**	to kiss
dîner	to dine	**employé** (m.)	employee
dire	to say	**en**	in
direct	direct	**en fait**	in fact
directeur, directrice	director	**enchanté**	delighted
		encore	again, still, yet

endormir (s')	to fall asleep	évidemment	of course,
énervé	irritated		obviously
enfance (f.)	childhood	évier (m.)	sink
enfant (m.)	child	éviter	to avoid
enfin	at last	exactement	exactly
enflé	swollen	examen (m.)	examination
enfuir (s')	to flee	excellent	excellent
enlever	to remove	exercice (m.)	exercise
ennuyer	to bore	expliquer	to explain
s'ennuyer	to be bored	exposition (f.)	exhibition
énormément	enormously		
ensemble	together	**F**	
entendre	to hear		
entre	between	fabuleux	fabulous
entrée (f.)	entrance,	facile	easy
	starter	facilement	easily
entreprise (f.)	company	facteur (m.)	postman
entrer	to come in	facture (f.)	invoice
envie (avoir)	to feel like	faim (avoir)	to be hungry
envoyer	to send	faire	to do/make
épaule (f.)	shoulder	faire mal (se)	to hurt
épinards (m.)	spinach		(a part of
éplucher	to peel		one's body)
époque (f.)	time	falloir	to need,
épouser	to marry		have to
épuisé	exhausted	famille (f.)	family
équitation (f.)	horse riding	fasciné	fascinated
escalade (f.)	climbing	fatigué	tired
escaliers (m.)	staircase, stairs	faux	wrong
escalope (f.)	escalope	favori	favourite
espagnol	Spanish	fax (m.)	fax
essayer	to try	félicitations (f.)	congratulations
est (m.)	east	femme (f.)	wife, woman
estomac (m.)	stomach	fermer	to close
étage (m.)	floor	fêter	to celebrate
état (m.)	state	feu (m.)	fire
été (m.)	summer	feuille (f.)	leaf
étranger	foreign	février (m.)	February
étranger (m.)	foreigner, abroad	fiche (f.)	form
être	to be	fièvre (f.)	fever
études (f.)	studies	fille (f.)	daughter, girl
étudiant (m.)	student	film (m.)	film

fils (m.)	son		gentil	nice, friendly
fin	thin		glace (f.)	ice cream
fin (f.)	end		glaçon (m.)	icicle, ice cube
finalement	finally, in the end		golf (m.)	golf
finir	to finish		gramme (m.)	gramme
fixer	arrange		grand	big, tall
flamme (f.)	flame		grand-chose	much
flan (m.)	flan		grand-mère (f.)	grandmother
flexible	flexible		grand-père (m.)	grandfather
fois (f.)	time		gratuit	free of charge
folklorique	outlandish, folkloric		grave	serious
			grenier (m.)	attic
fonctionnaire (m., f.)	Civil Servant		griller (faire)	to grill
			grippe (f.)	flu
football (m.)	football		gris	grey
forfait (m.)	package		guerre (f.)	war
forme (en)	fit, healthy		gym (f.)	gym
fortune (f.)	fortune			
fouler (se)	to sprain			
four (m.)	oven		**H**	
frais	fresh			
français	French		habillé	formal
frère (m.)	brother		habiter	to live
froid	cold		haché	minced
froisser	to crumple		haricots (m.)	beans
fromage (m.)	cheese		haut	high
fuite (f.)	leak		haut (en)	at the top
fumer	to smoke		herbes (f.)	herbs
			hésiter	to hesitate
			heure (à l')	on time
G			heure (de bonne)	early
			heure (f.)	hour
gagner	to win		heureusement	luckily
gants (m.)	gloves		heureux	happy
garage (m.)	garage		hideux	ugly
gare (f.)	station		hier	yesterday
gâteau (m.)	cake		hiver (m.)	winter
gauche (à)	left (on the)		hollandais	Dutch
gazeux	sparkling		homme (m.)	man
gel douche (m.)	shower gel		hôpital (m.)	hospital
genou (m.)	knee		horloge (f.)	clock
genre (m.)	type, kind		hôtel (m.)	hotel

housse de couette (f.)	quilt cover
huile (f.)	oil
huîtres (f.)	oysters

I

ici	here
idée (f.)	idea
il y a	there is, ago
imaginer (s')	to imagine
impatience (f.)	impatience
impérativement	imperatively
impossible	impossible
impressionnant	impressive
indien	Indian
indigestion (f.)	indigestion
industrie (f.)	industry
infirmier, -ière	nurse
informatique (f.)	IT
inquiéter (s')	to worry
insomnie (f.)	insomnia
instant (pour l')	for the moment
intellectuel (m.)	intellectual
intention (avoir l')	to intend
intéressant	interesting
intéresser (s')	to be interested
intérieur (m.)	interior, inside
internet (m.)	internet
invitation (f.)	invitation
inviter	to invite
italien	Italian

J

jamais	never
jambe (f.)	leg
jambon (m.)	ham
janvier (m.)	January
jardin (m.)	garden
jardinage (m.)	gardening

jaune	yellow
jaune d'œuf (m.)	egg yolk
jazz (m.)	jazz
jean (m.)	jeans
jeudi (m.)	Thursday
jeune	young
jogging (m.)	jogging
joli	nice
jouer	to play
jour (m.)	day
journal (m.)	a newspaper
journalisme (m.)	journalism
journée (f.)	day
juillet (m.)	July
juin (m.)	June
jupe (f.)	skirt
jus (m.)	juice
juste	just

K

karaté (m.)	karate
kilo (m.)	kilo
kilomètre (m.)	kilometre
kir (m.)	kir

L

là	there
lac (m.)	lake
laine (f.)	wool
laisser	to leave
lait (m.)	milk
lapin (m.)	rabbit
largement	largely, easily
lasagnes (f.)	lasagne
laurier (m.)	bay tree
le, la, les	the
légumes (m.)	vegetables
lendemain (m.)	following day
lequel, laquelle	which one
lessive (f.)	washing powder

lettre (f.)	letter		in . . .
leur, **leurs**	their	**malade**	ill
lever (**se**)	to get up	**malheureusement**	unfortunately
librairie (f.)	bookshop	**manger**	to eat
libre	free	**manquer**	to miss
light	diet (drink)	**manteau** (m.)	coat
lin (m.)	linen	**maquiller** (**se**)	to put on
liquide (**en**)	cash		make-up
lire	to read	**marche** (f.)	walking
liste (f.)	list	**marché** (m.)	market
lit (m.)	bed	**marcher**	to walk, work
litre (m.)	litre	**mardi** (m.)	Tuesday
livre (f.)	pound	**mari** (m.)	husband
livre (m.)	book	**marié**	married
location (f.)	rental	**marier** (**se**)	to get married
loin	far	**marine**	navy
loisirs (m.)	leisure	**marketing** (m.)	marketing
long	long	**marque** (f.)	label, make
long (**le**)	along	**marre** (**en avoir**)	to be fed up
louer	to rent	**marron**	brown
lui	him	**mars** (m.)	March
lumineux	bright	**match** (m.)	match
lundi (m.)	Monday	**matière** (f.)	material
luxe (m.)	luxury	**matin** (m.)	morning
		mayonnaise (f.)	mayonnaise
		mécanicien (m.)	mechanic
M		**médecin** (m.)	doctor
		médecine (f.)	medecine
madame	madam	**meilleur**	better
magasin (m.)	shop	**mélanger**	to mix
magnifique	beautiful,	**membre** (m.)	member
	spendid	**ménage** (m.)	housework
mai (m.)	May	**menthe** (f.)	mint
maillot de bains	swimming	**merci**	thank you
(m.)	costume	**mercredi** (m.)	Wednesday
maintenant	now	**mère** (f.)	mother
maire (m.)	mayor	**merguez** (f.)	merguez
mairie (f.)	town hall	**message** (m.)	message
mais	but	**métier** (m.)	profession
maison (f.)	house	**mètre** (m.)	metre
mal (**avoir du**)	to find it	**mettre**	to put
	difficult	**meublé**	furnished
mal à (**avoir**)	to feel pain		

midi	12 noon	**naître**	to be born
miel (m.)	honey	**nappe** (f.)	tablecloth
mieux	better, best	**nationalité** (f.)	nationality
mignon	cute	**naturel**	natural
mijoter (**faire**)	to simmer	**navré**	sorry
minéral	mineral	**négliger**	to neglect
minuit	midnight	**neiger**	to snow
minute (m.)	minute	**neuf**	new
mélange (m.)	mixture	**neveu** (m.)	nephew
modèle (m.)	model	**nièce** (f.)	niece
moderne	modern	**noir**	black, dark
moi	me	**nom** (m.)	name
moins	less	**nord** (m.)	north
moins (**au**)	at least	**normalement**	normally
mois (m.)	month	**notaire** (m., f.)	solicitor
moment (m.)	moment	**notre, nos**	our
mon, ma, mes	my	**nourriture** (f.)	food
mondial	world, global	**nouveau**	new
monnaie (f.)	currency, change	**nouvelles** (f.)	news
monsieur (m.)	sir	**novembre** (m.)	November
montagne (f.)	mountain	**nuit** (f.)	night
monter	to go up	**nul**	non-existent,
montre (f.)	watch		useless
montrer	to show	**numéro** (m.)	number
monument (m.)	monument	**nylon** (m.)	nylon
morceau (m.)	piece		
moule (m.)	baking dish		
moules (f.)	mussels	**O**	
mourir	to die		
moussaka (f.)	moussaka	**objet** (m.)	object
moutarde (f.)	mustard	**obtenir**	to obtain
moyen	medium	**occupé**	busy
moyens	to be able to	**occuper** (**s'**)	to look after
(**avoir les**)	afford	**octobre** (m.)	October
musée (m.)	museum	**œuf** (m.)	egg
musicien, -ienne	musician	**œuvre d'art** (f.)	work of art
musique (f.)	music	**Office du**	tourist office
		Tourisme (m.)	
		offre (f.)	offer
N		**offrir**	to offer
		oignon (m.)	onion
nager	to swim	**olive** (f.)	olive
naissance (f.)	birth	**oncle** (m.)	uncle

orage (m.)	storm	**passer**	to spend, to go past
orange (f.)	orange		
organiser	to organise	**passer** (se)	to take place
original	original	**passe-temps** (m.)	hobby
orteil (m.)	toe	**pâté** (m.)	paté
où	where	**pâtisserie** (f.)	cake, pâtisserie
oublier	to forget, leave behind	**pavé**	paved
		pays (m.)	country
ouest (m.)	west	**peau** (f.)	skin
		pêche (f.)	fishing, peach
		peine	don't bother
P		**(ce n'est pas la)**	
		peinture (f.)	painting
pain (m.)	bread	**pelouse** (f.)	lawn
pain de mie (m.)	sandwich loaf	**pendant**	for
paire (f.)	pair	**penser**	to think
paix (f.)	peace	**perdre**	to lose
palmier (m.)	palm tree	**père** (m.)	father
pamplemousse (m.)	grapefruit	**permettre** (se)	allow
		permis de conduire (m.)	driving licence
panorama (m.)	view, panorama		
panoramique	panoramic	**persil** (m.)	parsley
pantalon (m.)	trousers	**personne** (f.)	person, no one
papeterie (f.)	stationery	**peser** (se)	to weigh oneself
papier (m.)	paper	**petit**	small
papier toilettes (m.)	toilet paper	**petit déjeuner** (m.)	breakfast
paprika (m.)	paprika	**peu** (un)	little, a little
paquet (m.)	paquet	**peur** (avoir)	to be scared
parapluie (m.)	umbrella	**peut-être**	maybe
parce que	because	**pharmacie** (f.)	chemist
pare-brise (m.)	windscreen	**photo** (f.)	photograph
pareillement	in the same way	**pièce** (f.)	coin, room
		pièce d'identité (f.)	ID
parent (m.)	parent		
parfait	perfect	**pied** (à) (m.)	foot (on)
parfum (m.)	perfume	**piloter**	to pilot
parking (m.)	car park	**pincée** (f.)	pinch
parler	to talk	**piscine** (f.)	swimming pool
part (de leur)	on their behalf	**pizzeria** (f.)	pizzeria
partir	to leave, go	**place** (f.)	square, room
passeport (m.)	passport	**plage** (f.)	beach

plaire	to be liked	**présenter**	to present,
plaisanter	to joke		to introduce
plaisir (m.)	pleasure	**presque**	nearly
plan (m.)	map	**pression** (f.)	draught (beer)
planche à	ironing board	**prêt**	ready
repasser (f.)		**printanier**	spring-like
plancher (m.)	wooden floor	**printemps** (m.)	spring
plante (f.)	plant	**prix** (m.)	price
planter	to plant	**problème** (m.)	problem
plaque (f.)	packet, bar	**prochain**	next
pleuvoir	to rain	**professeur** (m.)	teacher
plombier (m.)	plumber	**profession** (f.)	profession
pluie (f.)	rain	**projet** (m.)	plan, project
plus (**ne**)	more, longer	**promener** (**se**)	to go for a
	(no)		walk
plutôt	rather	**promotion** (**en**)	on special offer
poids (m.)	weight	**proposer**	to propose
poignet (m.)	wrist	**provisions** (f.)	food supplies
pointure (f.)	size	**prudent**	careful
poisson (m.)	fish	**pub** (m.)	pub
poivre (m.)	pepper	**public**	public
poivrer	to pepper	**puis**	then
pollution (f.)	pollution	**pull** (m.)	jumper
pomme (f.)	apple		
pont (m.)	bridge	**Q**	
porc (m.)	pork		
portable (m.)	mobile	**quand**	when
poser	to put	**quand même**	still
poste (f.)	post office	**quart** (m.)	quarter
potentiel	potential	**quartier** (m.)	quarter, area
pour	for, in order to	**que**	what, that,
pourquoi	why		which, who,
pourtant	yet		whom
pouvoir	to be able to,	**quel**	which, what
	can	**quelque chose**	something
pratique	convenient	**quelquefois**	sometimes
préchauffer	to preheat	**quelques**	a few, some
préférer	to prefer	**quelqu'un**	someone
premier	first	**qui**	who
prendre	to take	**quitter** (**ne pas**)	to leave,
préparer	to prepare		hold on
prescrire	to prescribe	**quoi**	what

R

raccrocher	to hang up
raconter	to tell
radio (f.)	radio
raison (avoir)	to be right
raisonnable	reasonable
ramener	to bring back (person or animal)
rangée (f.)	a line
ranger	to store, tidy up
rapide	fast
rappeler (se)	to call back, to remember
rapport (m.)	report
rapporter	to bring back (inanimate object)
rare	rare
raser (se)	to shave
rassuré	reassured
ratatouille (f.)	ratatouille
raté	failed
ravi	delighted
rayon (m.)	section
rayures (f.)	stripes
recevoir	to receive
réclame (en)	on special offer
recyclage (m.)	recycling
refaire	to redo
réfléchir	to think
refuser	to refuse
régaler (se)	to enjoy a lot
regarder	to watch, look
régime (m.)	diet
région (f.)	region
regretter	to regret
régulièrement	regularly
relaxation (f.)	relaxation
remarquer	to notice
remercier	to thank

renard (m.)	fox
rendez-vous (m.)	appointment
rénovations (f.)	renovations
rénover	to renovate
rentrer	to come back
réparations (f.)	repairs
réparer	to repair
repasser	to iron
répondeur (m.)	answerphone
répondre	to answer
réponse (f.)	answer
reposer (se)	to rest
représentant, -e	representative
réservation (f.)	reservation
réserver	to book
restaurant (m.)	restaurant
rester	to stay
résultat (m.)	result
retard (m.) **(en)**	delay, late
retirer	to withdraw
retour (m.)	return
retourner	to return, go back
retraité	retired
retraite (à la)	retired
retrouver (se)	to find again, meet
réunion (f.)	meeting
réussir	to succeed
réveiller (se)	to wake up
revenir	to come back, brown
revenu (m.)	income
rez-de-chaussée (m.)	ground floor
rhume (m.)	cold
rien	nothing
rire	to laugh
risquer	to risk, might
robe (f.)	dress
romain	Roman
romaine (f.)	cos lettuce

rose	pink	**signer**	to sign
rouge	red	**s'il vous plaît**	please
rouler	to drive, go	**simple**	single, simple
route (f.)	road	**situer (se)**	to be situated
rue (f.)	street	**société** (f.)	company
rugby (m.)	rugby	**sœur** (f.)	sister
russe	Russian	**sofa** (m.)	sofa
		soie (f.)	silk
S		**soif (avoir)**	to be thirsty
		soir (m.)	evening
sainement	in a healthy way	**soirée** (f.)	evening
salade (f.)	salad, lettuce	**solde (en)**	sale price
saler	to salt	**soleil** (m.)	sun
salle (f.)	room	**solution** (f.)	solution
salle de bains	bathroom	**somnifères** (m.)	sleeping tablets
(f.)		**son, sa, ses**	his, her
salon (m.)	lounge, salon	**sonnette** (f.)	doorbell
salut	hi	**sortir**	to leave, go
samedi (m.)	Saturday		out
santé (f.)	health	**soucis** (m.)	worries
saucisson (m.)	dried pork	**souhaiter**	to wish
	sausage	**soupe** (f.)	soup
saumon (m.)	salmon	**sous**	under
sauna (m.)	sauna	**sous-sol** (m.)	basement
savoir	to know	**sous-vêtements**	underwear
séchoir (m.)	clothes-horse	(m.)	
secrétaire (m., f.)	secretary	**souvenir (se)**	to remember
séjour (m.)	stay, living	**souvenirs** (m.)	memories
	room	**souvent**	often
sel (m.)	salt	**spécial**	special
sélection (f.)	selection	**sport** (m.)	sport
semaine (f.)	week	**sportif**	sporty
sentir (se)	to feel, smell	**squash** (m.)	squash
séparément	separately	**steak** (m.)	steak
septembre (m.)	September	**stocker**	to stock
sérieux	serious	**stressé**	stressed
serveur, -euse	waiter	**studio** (m.)	studio
servir	to serve	**sud** (m.)	south
seul	alone	**suffire**	to be enough
shopping (m.)	shopping	**suggérer**	to suggest
short (m.)	shorts	**suivre**	to follow
si	yes, if	**super**	super, wonderful

supermarché (m.)	supermarket	**tomate** (f.)	tomato
sur	on	**tomber**	to fall
surface habitable (f.)	surface area	**ton, ta, tes**	your
		tort (avoir)	to be wrong
surgelés (m.)	frozen food	**toujours**	always, still
surprenant	surprising	**tour** (f.)	tower
sympathique	nice, friendly	**touristique**	touristy
		tourner	to turn
		tous, toutes	all, every
T		**tout**	everything
		tout à coup	suddenly
table (f.)	table	**tout compris**	all included
taille (f.)	size	**tout de suite**	straight away
talon (m.)	heel	**traditionnel**	traditional
tango (m.)	tango	**train** (m.)	train
tante (f.)	aunt	**traiter**	to deal
taper	to type	**tranche** (f.)	slice
tard	late	**transpirer**	to perspire
tarte (f.)	pie	**transports**	public
taxi (m.)	taxi	**publics** (m.)	transport
téléphone (m.)	telephone	**travail** (m.)	work
téléphoner	to phone	**travailler**	to work
télévision (f.)	television	**travaux** (m.)	works
tellement	so	**traverser**	to cross
température (f.)	temperature	**trop**	too much
temps (en même)	at the same time	**trouver (se)**	to find, be found
temps (m.)	time, weather	**truite** (f.)	trout
tennis (m.)	tennis	**TVA** (f.)	VAT
tension (f.)	blood pressure		
tenter	to tempt	**U**	
terminer	to finish		
terrain (m.)	land	**un, une**	a
terrasse (f.)	terrace	**uni** (m.)	plain
théâtre (m.)	theatre		
théoriquement	theoretically	**V**	
thon (m.)	tuna		
thym (m.)	thyme	**vacances** (f.)	holidays
toi	you	**vaisselle** (f.)	crockery, washing-up
toile (f.)	painting	**valise** (f.)	suitcase
toilettes (f.)	toilets	**vanille** (f.)	vanilla
toit (m.)	roof	**vase** (m.)	vase

veau (m.)	veal	**violet**	purple, violet
vélo (m.)	a bicycle, cycling	**visibilité** (f.)	visibility
velours (m.)	velvet	**visiter**	visit
vendeur, -euse	salesman	**vitrine** (f.)	shop window
vendre	to sell	**vivre**	to live
vendredi (m.)	Friday	**voilà**	there you are
venir	to come	**voile** (f.)	sailing
venir de	to have just	**voir**	to see
vent (m.)	wind	**voiture** (f.)	car
ventre (m.)	tummy	**vol** (m.)	flight
verre (m.)	glass, drink	**votre, vos**	your
vers	around, towards	**vouloir**	to want
verser	to pour	**voyage** (m.)	trip, travel
vert	green	**voyager**	to travel
veste (f.)	cardigan, jacket	**vrai**	right
vêtements (m.)	clothes	**vraiment**	really
vétuste	decrepit, showing its age	**vue** (f.)	sight, view

W

week-end (m.)	weekend
whisky (m.)	whisky

viande (f.)	meat		
vie (f.)	life		
vieil, vieux	old		
village (m.)	village		
ville (f.)	town hall		
vin (m.)	wine		
vinaigre (m.)	vinegar		
violent	violent		

Y

y	there
yaourt (m.)	yoghurt
yoga (m.)	yoga

Grammar index

This index will help you to locate topics, grammar points, and so on. The references opposite each item are to the unit number.

Topic and functions index

Related titles from Routledge

Colloquial French 2

Elspeth Broady

Do you know French already and want to go a stage further? If you're planning a visit to France, need to brush up your French for work, or are simply doing a course, Colloquial French 2 is the ideal way to refresh your knowledge of the language and to extend your skills.

Colloquial French 2 is designed to help those involved in self-study, and structured to give you the opportunity to listen to and read lots of modern, everyday French. It has been developed to work systematically on reinforcing and extending your grasp of French grammar and vocabulary.

Key features of Colloquial French 2 include:

- a broad range of everyday situations, focusing on France and the wider francophone world
- revision material to help consolidate and build up your basics
- a wide range of contemporary documents
- spoken and written exercises in each unit
- highlighted key structures and phrases, a grammar reference and detailed answer keys
- supplementary exercises and French language web links at www.routledge.com/cw/colloquials

Audio material to accompany the course is available to download freely in MP3 format from www.routledge.com/cw/colloquials. Recorded by native speakers, the audio material features the dialogues and texts from the book and will help develop your listening and pronunciation skills.

Pbk: 978-1-138-95012-2

Available at all good bookshops
For ordering and further information please visit:
www.routledge.com